100 Ways to Say I Love You

Handmade Gifts and Heartfelt Expressions

Jane LaFerla

Lark Books

Contents by Materials or Techniques

Handmade Gifts

Introduction

Loving and giving are as forever linked as hugs and kisses, hearts and flowers, or slow dancing and love songs. Every time you say "I love you," you're expressing a world of emotion. By giving the right gift to someone you love, you're showing you care by capturing the essence of your relationship in a tangible, touchable way.

The true art in giving a gift of love is finding a meaningful memento. We've all agonized over selecting just the right object to give someone we love. When you do this, you're looking for something more than a mere object, you're questing for a symbol of the special love you share with that person since a gift of love is a form of secret code between you and the recipient. Nothing is more fun than watching the face of someone you love light up with a smile of recognition when they get the underlying message or thought behind the gift they've just received.

Handmade gifts bring an extra measure of thoughtfulness. When you fashion a gift by hand, via your heart, you're infusing that gift with your loving touch. Though unseen, this sentiment is rarely lost in that profound moment when the receiver realizes you actually made this for them!

With handmade gifts, you're not only giving your heart away but your creativity, talents, and time as well. You can personalize handmade gifts to incorporate any symbols that are particularly meaningful to your relationship. You can slip in the shells you found at the beach last summer, the feather you picked up on a hike, present a favorite flower, write a special phrase, or use a photo you both treasure.

Gifts from the heart are not always objects but can also be expressions of love. My own personal favorite is, "Honey, I know you've been busy, so what if I cook tonight?" A love song couldn't be sweeter music to my ears! A gift of time for a harried mother, a meal for someone unable to cook, a tedious chore done for another—all of these can be more valuable than gold.

This book will provide you with 100 ways to say I love you any time throughout the year. You'll find 75 gifts to make and 25 ideas for heartfelt expressions for spouses, significant others, siblings, parents, children, grandchildren, neighbors, and pets. Whether you're looking for a gift to mark a formal occasion, or for the right way to show someone you care "just because," *100 Ways to Say I Love You* will help you give a unique gift from the heart.

We urge you to try something new! If you've never thought of beading, you may surprise yourself when you master the peyote stitch so you can complete a project you like. Perhaps you've been waiting for the chance to experiment with the beautiful handmade papers you've admired in the art-supply shop, or are looking for a way to learn about pressed flowers, soap-making, or simple mosaics. We hope this book will not only inspire you with gift ideas but will also provide you with the opportunity to learn—which is, after all, the best gift we can give to you!

HOW TO USE THIS BOOK

The projects in this book represent a range of materials and techniques. Whether you're a novice or a more experienced crafter, you'll find projects to match your skill level. When space permits, the book includes basic information on techniques. However, if you do not find the information you need to get started, please refer to books about that particular craft.

Before you begin a project, read the instructions through carefully. If you are unsure about a step, practice on a scrap of material until you feel comfortable with the technique.

Some projects include patterns, templates, or charts which are found in their own section in the back of the book. Project directions will give you the page number where you can find the corresponding pattern. If necessary, directions for enlarging the pattern when you photocopy it will be included.

Hearty Hug and Hugs & Kisses Pillows

Designer Linda Kaiser-Bonin says, "The passion and excitement that surrounds how you feel about those you love should be reflected in the choice of colors you use for these whimsical designs."

MATERIALS

For each design you will need:

¼ yard (23 cm) of fabric for the top panel

Bright-colored fabric scraps for appliqués and seam binding

Fusible web

⅛ yard (11.5 cm) of fabric for the border

17 x 13" (43 x 33 cm) quilt batting

½ yard (45.5 cm) of fabric for the backing

Embroidery floss

TOOLS

Scissors

Pencil

Needle

Sewing machine

Iron

GENERAL INSTRUCTIONS

Patterns for the appliqués are on page 126.

1. Cut the ¼-yard (23-cm) fabric for the top panel to measure 8½ x 12½" (21.5 x 31.5 cm).

2. Using the patterns on page 126, transfer the designs for the appliqués onto the bright-colored fabric scraps, then cut out.

3. Trace and cut the same appliqué shapes from the fusible web. Trim the outside edge of the fusible web

shapes so they are slightly smaller than the bright-colored shaped.

4. Position the shapes cut from the fusible web on the top panel fabric. Place the appliqué shapes cut from the fabric scraps on the corresponding fusible-web shapes. Following the fusible-web instructions, iron the appliqués onto the fabric.

Once you've completed Step 4 for Hearty Hug and Step 5 for Hugs and Kisses, proceed with Step 5 of the General Instructions.

For Hearty Hug:

1. From the border fabric, cut two strips, size 2½ x 12½" (6.5 x 31.5 cm), and two strips size 2½ x 8½" (6.5 x 21. 5 cm).

2. From the same fabric you used for the hand appliqué, cut four 2½" (6.5 cm) squares.

3. Using a ½" (1.5 cm) seam allowance, sew one 2½" (6.5 cm) square to each end of both 12½" (31.5 cm) strips.

4. Sew the shorter 2½ x 8½" (6.5 x 21.5 cm) strips to the short ends of the top panel fabric, then sew the longer strips made in Step 3 to the long ends of the top panel fabric.

For Hugs & Kisses:

1. For the border, cut three 1 x 45" (2.5 x 114.5 cm) strips from a fabric that will match the colors of the embroidery floss you will use for the buttonhole stitch in Step 6 of the General Instructions.

2. Sew the three strips together lengthwise, then cut these into 1" (2.5 cm) wide rectangles (mix up the colors for a random color scheme).

3. Sew these rectangles together, using 13 rectangles for the two short sides and 20 rectangles for the two long sides.

4. Cut four 2" (5 cm) squares of contrasting fabric and sew one to each of the corners of the two long patchwork strips you made in Step 3.

5. Sew the short patchwork strips to the short sides of the top panel fabric, and the long patchwork strips to the long sides of the top panel fabric.

GENERAL INSTRUCTIONS cont.

5. From the backing fabric, cut one piece 17 x 13" (43 x 33 cm). From the quilt batting, cut a piece the same size as the backing fabric. Layer the backing, batting, and top panel, with appliqués facing up, then baste all layers together.

6. Use three strands of embroidery floss to hand embroider a buttonhole stitch around the appliqué edges and the corner squares on each top, stitching through the three layers of fabric from Step 5.

7. For the pillow backs, cut one piece of fabric 12½ x 12½" (31.5 cm x 31.5 cm). Fold one edge under ½" (1.5 cm), then fold under again 2" (5 cm) and hem.

8. Cut one piece of fabric 10½ x 12½" (26.5 x 31.5 cm). Fold one 12½" (31.5 cm) edge under ½" (1.5 cm) and hem.

9. Overlap the finished edges of the two rectangles made in Steps 7 and 8, laying the rectangle with the 2" (5 cm) hem on top. Lay both pieces right side down.

10. With its right side up, lay the top panel over the two lapped back pieces, adjusting until all raw edges are even. Pin all layers together.

11. You can use purchased 2" (5 cm) wide seam binding for your binding strips, or make your own seam binding from the bright-colored scraps. To make your own, sew three 24" (61 cm) long strips together using bias (diagonal) seams.

12. Turn both long edges of the binding under ¼" (.5 cm) with wrong sides together and press. Press the binding strips in half, wrong sides together.

13. Beginning at the center of one of the long sides of the pillow, position the seam binding with one half of its width on either side of the pillow's raw edges. Stitch one edge of the binding along its ¼" (.5 cm) foldline through all layers of the top and back. Turn the binding to the back, turning under at the ¼" (.5 cm) foldline and whipstitch in place.

Tip: You can make a wall hanging from your quilted top panel. Simply use a binding strip to finish the raw edges of your panel. Cut a 6½ x 12½" (16.5 x 31.5 cm) fabric rectangle. Hem the short edges, then sew into a tube and turn. (This will be your "sleeve" for the hanging rod.) Whipstitch the tube to the back of the quilt.

Designer: Linda Kaiser-Bonin

Love Letter Envelopes

With these artistic envelopes, your gift of love will be a treat for the eyes as well as the heart. Designer Nicole Tuggle says, "Since letter writing is an art, the envelope should reflect the same thought and care you use in choosing your words."

3

MATERIALS

Cardboard (old boxes work great!), mat board, or sturdy poster board

Handmade paper of various colors and textures

Envelope, any size (handmade is preferred)

Charms, trinkets, old jewelry, any object of significance or appeal

Craft glue

Strong quick-drying glue

TOOLS

Craft Knife

Scissors

Ruler

Pencil

Hot glue gun and glue sticks

INSTRUCTIONS

1. With the craft knife, cut two rectangles of equal size from the cardboard. The size of the envelope will determine the size of board.

2. Using the cardboard as a pattern, lay it on the handmade paper. Measure ½" (1.5 cm) from the edges of the cardboard, then mark this measurement all the way around for your cutting lines. Cut out two pieces from the handmade paper.

3. Coat one side of each piece of cardboard with the craft glue. Center the paper, one sheet each, on both pieces of cardboard, leaving a ½" (1.5) border around the edges.

4. There are various ways of folding the paper for a neat finish —the one shown in the figure below is the easiest. Cut straight in from the outer edges of the paper. Cut the side paper at an angle as shown. Glue each side and press it to the cardboard, smoothing it to make it as flush as possible.

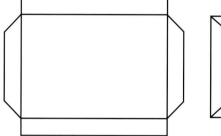 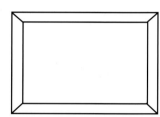

5. Cut two pieces of handmade paper that are large enough to overlap the glued edges by at least ¼" (.5 cm). Make sure the paper is large enough to cover any blank board, but small enough to show a border of the paper used to cover the cardboard. Glue one piece to each inside surface of the covered cardboard panel.

6. To connect both rectangles, use a piece of strong but flexible paper or ribbon. Cut the ribbon or paper to a piece that is 1"- 2" (2.5 - 5 cm) wide and the exact length of the edges of the cardboard panels that will be connected.

7. Place the two rectangles together, side by side, with right sides (outside) down. It is important that the edges that will be connected are touching. If you leave a space between the panels, the connection will be weak and wobbly.

8. Fully coat one side of the paper or ribbon connector strip with the strong quick-drying glue and firmly affix to the inside edges of the cardboard panels. Before the glue dries, fold the two rectangles together to make sure they will close well.

9. Attach your envelope to the inside of your card by coating the back of the envelope with glue. You may want to cut off the envelope flap so the receiver will see the letter waiting inside.

10. Personalize the card by decorating it anyway you want—variations are only limited by your imagination! Use hot glue to attach old jewelry pieces or small metal trinkets to the cover. A small photocopied image is a nice alternative. Decorating the inside of the card also offers many possibilities. Keep the inside of the card that faces the envelope blank, or use it as a space for a poem or picture. Just make sure that whatever you put on the inside of the card is flat so it will not prevent the card from closing.

Variation: Design your card so it opens in the center. Cut two pieces of cardboard the same size, then cut one of the pieces in half. Follow the same steps for covering and attaching the panels and decorating.

Designer: Nicole Tuggle

4 Write a Love Letter

*E*ven though we live in a world of instant communi-
cation—where a phone call from across the globe
is as crystal-clear as a call from down the block,
where on-line cyber dates are commonplace, where
a marriage proposal can be faxed anywhere in
the world—nothing is as romantic as a good
old-fashioned love letter.

What a gift to find your grandmother's or parents'
love letters. In bundles of yellowed stationery tied
with faded ribbons, or in a shoe box full of envelopes
with postmarks from across the country or the world,
are hidden bits of family history otherwise unspoken.
More than a quaint record of an era, an old love
letter is a treasure map, showing us how to reach
the heart of another.

If you've dismissed the idea of writing love letters
with thoughts of inadequate skills, please reconsider.
At the core of every love letter is the abandon to
freely speak your heart, no matter what form it
takes. Remember—love is mightier than the rules
of grammar! Set your preconceived ideas aside,
and you'll be surprised at the eloquent writing
that will flow from your pen.

For inspiration, read one of the many wonderful
anthologies of great love letters. Even though these
are written by some of the world's best-known
writers, you'll immediately find similarities to your
own feelings of love and romance, attesting to the
universality of this complex human emotion.

If you need help to put you in the mood, find
a special stationery, turn on the love songs,
compose by candlelight, write with a fountain pen,
and close the letter with sealing wax. Not only will
you be chronicling your love, you may be creating
treasured family memories that will be discovered
by future generations.

Doily Design T-Shirt

*H*eat-transfer dyes and fabric crayons
allow you to easily transfer
color designs to just about any
fabric surface. The designer chose
a polyester T-shirt in a style that's popular
with teenage girls, and created a lacy
mandala-inspired piece of "heart" work.

5

Designer: Ellen Zahorec

MATERIALS

Paper doily

Medium-weight plain paper

Heat-transfer dyes or fabric crayons, available in most craft and fabric stores

Polyester T-shirt (a cotton or cotton blend shirt works as well)

TOOLS

Scissors

Old newspapers or blank newsprint

Iron

INSTRUCTIONS

1. To make the patterns for your design, cut the doilies and arrange them into a design of your choice (or, if desired, you can leave the doily as is). If you don't have a doily, you can fold and cut paper to create lacy paper snowflakes. Cut paper hearts out of plain paper.

2. Use the heat-transfer dyes or fabric crayons to paint or color your paper design and the cut-out hearts.

3. Heat your iron, being careful to avoid heating it to a temperature that is too high. For best results, follow the guidelines provided by the manufacturers of the dyes and crayons.

4. Place a few sheets of old newspaper or blank newsprint inside the shirt.

5. Turn the painted/colored doilies and papers face down onto the right side of the fabric, positioning the patterns where you want them.

6. Place a few sheets of old newspaper or blank newsprint over the top of the paper patterns. Iron until the color transfers. Remove the paper.

7. The designs are permanent. To launder the shirt, follow the dye or crayon manufacturer's instructions.

6 *Teenagers and College Students*

Even if you don't know the latest trends or current popular bands, you can give gifts that will please discriminating teenagers and college students. While requests for money seem to be the all-time favorite answer when you ask this age group what they want for a gift, there are other more imaginative ways to show you love them.

Coupon books and gift certificates from fast-food restaurants, movie theaters, and video-rental or music stores will always be used. For a student with a car, offer coupons to a car wash or for a year's worth of oil changes from a local garage. Find and give a year's magazine subscription pertaining to their special interests such as surfing, snow boarding, photography, soccer, fashion, computers, or cars.

Trade chores for privileges, such as cleaning the basement or doing yard work in exchange for a one-hour extension on a curfew, doing the weekly family laundry or shopping for two months in exchange for prom extras such as formal photos, special flowers, or a manicure. For a teenager juggling school and a job, give them the gift of time by offering a homemade coupon book good for 10 errands or household chores.

College students who are away from home look forward to hearing from you. While e-mail via computer can help you communicate every day, nothing replaces the anticipation of opening an envelope or package from home. Any item a budgeting college student doesn't have to buy themselves is money in their pocket. Send them a care package with favorite "luxury" toiletries, a preferred but expensive shampoo, cologne, soap, or lotion. Enclose a few favorite snacks, homemade cookies, packages of microwave popcorn, and soup mix for late-night study. Put together a box of supplies that they always use such as laundry detergent, fabric softener, bleach, and a few rolls of coins for the washers, dryers, and vending machines. Send a disposable camera, so they can take snapshots of their dorm, roommates, or special events to share with you when they're home.

Women's Message Pillow

Τhe lacy pocket in this satin pillow is perfect for holding a seductive love note. Lay it on someone's pillow and see what can happen.

Instructions for Women's Sachets on page 18

MATERIALS

Paper

White satin

Black lace—at least 8" (20.5 cm) wide x 11" (28 cm) long

Polyester pillow fill

2 yds. (1.8 m) black decorative cord

2 red silk-ribbon roses

1 yd. (.9 m) of 2" (5 cm) wide green ribbon

2 yds. (1.8 m) of ⅝" (1.6 cm) wide green ribbon

3 small silk rosebuds, two pink and one red

1 yd. (.9 m) of 1½" (4 cm) pink ribbon

TOOLS

Scissors

Sewing machine

Needles and thread

INSTRUCTIONS

1. Draw or trace a heart shape on paper and cut it out. The heart shape for this pillow measures 8" (20.5 cm) tall by 10½" (26.5 cm) wide.

2. From this pattern, cut two hearts out of the satin.

3. Fold the remaining satin crosswise so it is approximately 8" (20.5 cm) deep by 12" (30.5 cm) wide.

4. Place the heart pattern made in Step 1 over the folded satin. Extend the top of the heart approximately 2½" (6.5 cm) from the top of the folded edge and pin through both layers of satin. Cut out the lower portion of the heart through the two layers (see Figure 1). Keep this partial heart shape folded on the fold line.

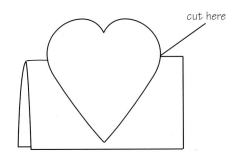

cut here

FIGURE 1

5. Lay the black lace over the folded satin. If the lace has a scalloped edge, extend it slightly over the fold of the satin. With black thread on the sewing machine, stitch the black lace through both layers of satin along the folded edge. Trim the lace to the heart shape. This becomes the pocket.

6. Baste the pocket to the right side of one of the satin hearts cut in Step 2.

7. Place the other satin heart over it, right sides together, and stitch a ⅜" (1 cm) seam along the edges of the heart, leaving an opening to turn.

8. Trim the seams and clip the curves. Turn right side out.

9. Press the edges, then stuff the heart with polyester pillow filling. Slip stitch the opening.

10. Find the center point of the black cord. Place this point at the bottom point of the heart and pin. Sew the cord by hand to the edges of the heart to cover the seamlines. Leave the ends of the cord, which will meet at the center top of the heart, to dangle.

11. Make or purchase two red silk-ribbon roses.

12. To make the leaves, cut the 2" (5 cm) wide green ribbon into four equal pieces. Take one piece and fold each of its ends over the center, then down. Fold again into the center (see Figure 2). Repeat with the other pieces of green ribbon.

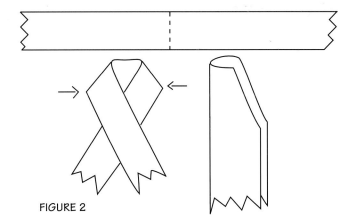

FIGURE 2

13. Sew two leaves to the sides of each red silk rose.

14. Sew one silk rose with leaves to the left front center of the heart and one silk rose to right back center of heart.

15. Gather up the ⅝" (1.6 cm) wide green ribbon into seven bow loops; make one side of the bow with short loops, the other side of the bow with longer loops. Once you finish making the loops, there should be ends left on the bow.

16. Sew the bow onto the center top of the heart between the roses. Position the shorter bow loops toward the front of the heart and the longer bow loops toward the back. The ends of the bow should trail over the front and back of the heart.

17. Arrange the pink and red silk rosebuds to your liking. Join them together by wrapping thread or tape around their stems close to the rosebuds. Trim the stems away. Sew the rosebuds to the center front of the heart.

18. Make a bow with the 1½" (4 cm) pink ribbon with one loop slightly longer than the other. Put the slightly longer loop toward the back of the heart, and sew the bow to the center of the heart. Adjust the loops and trailing ends of this bow until you like the look. Trim the ends of the trailers so they end at different points.

19. Take the ends of the black cord from Step 10 and loop them, tying the loops into themselves as you go. Arrange as you please.

Designer: Lisa Sanders

Women's Sachets

Soft, lacy sachets make a thoughtful gift for a friend (mother, sister, or daughter) who appreciates a feminine touch. Choose a scent to match her personality—sunny, flowery, or woodsy. Every time she opens her drawer, she'll be reminded of your friendship.

Photo on page 16

MATERIALS
Lace

Satin fabric

Polyester pillow fill

Scent pellets or potpourri

TOOLS
Scissors

Thread

Pins

INSTRUCTIONS

Variation A: Allover Lace Sachet

1. Cut a rectangle of lace 4¾ x 8¾" (12 x 22 cm).

2. Fold the rectangle in half with right sides together to make a square.

3. Using a ⅜" (1 cm) seam allowance, stitch around the edges, leaving a small opening to turn.

4. Turn sachet right side out.

5. Fill with polyester fill.

6. Using the edge of one scissor blade, cut a slit pocket into the polyester filling.

7. Insert scent pellets or potpourri into the slit pocket.

8. Slip stitch the opening closed.

Variation B: Satin and Lace Sachet

1. Measure the length and width of the lace motif you will use. For this design, it's 5" long x 4½" wide (12.5 x 11.5 cm).

2. Cut a rectangle of satin about 1" (2.5 cm) wider and two times plus 2" (5 cm) longer than the lace. For this design, the measurement is 5¼" wide x 12" long (13.5 x 30.5 cm).

3. Fold the rectangle in half and mark the foldline with pins.

4. Open the rectangle and position the lace motif on one half of the rectangle, trying to keep it evenly spaced from all edges.

5. Pin the lace in place, pinning approximately every ¾" (2 cm) along the edges of the lace motif.

6. Using a fine zigzag stitch, sew the lace to the satin.

7. Carefully cut the satin out from behind the lace, cutting up to ⅛" (.3 cm) from the edge of the zigzag stitching. Use small scissors and cut slowly and carefully to avoid cutting through the lace. Press.

8. Fold the rectangle in half with the right sides together, and using a ⅜" (1 cm) seam allowance, stitch around the edges, leaving a small opening to turn. Turn right side out.

9. Follow Steps 5-8 for Variation A.

Tip: For best results, choose a lace with a motif that has closed edges. If you choose a lace intended for appliqué, you may not be able to cut the satin away from behind the lace.

Designer: Lisa Sanders

Decoupage Votive Candles

These decorated votives are especially nice to give someone as a little gift to remind them how you feel. They're easy to make, and can also be used in centerpieces for parties celebrating an engagement, anniversary, or wedding.

9

Instructions for the Paper Candle Lantern are on page 20

MATERIALS

Tall clear-glass votive candle

Rice paper—or paper that is thin and slightly transparent, such as tissue paper

Spray adhesive, suitable for glass

Decorative paper

Craft glue

Paper or cloth ribbon

Dried flowers

Bath or Massage Oils

By making your own bath and massage oils, you know you're using only the purest ingredients—very important when you're caring for the skin of someone you love. The indulgent luxury of combining sweet almond oil with scented essential oils provides a sensuous bath or massage experience and makes a most welcome gift.

INGREDIENTS

Dried flowers—the oils shown feature rose and lavender

Sweet almond oil

Essential oil in scent of your choice

Vitamin E—optional

Safflower oil—optional

In addition you will need:

Clean, dry, clear-glass (not opaque) bottles

Paraffin wax—optional

1. Use flowers that are completely dry and natural. Flowers used in commercial potpourri are not suitable for this recipe. Make sure the flowers are clean—you don't want any debris in your massage oil.

2. Place the flowers in the clean, dry bottle. Do not fill the bottle full of flowers. You are adding the flowers for visual appeal since dried flowers are incapable of scenting the oil.

3 Blend the sweet almond oil with the essential oil in a scent of your choice. Sweet almond oil is an expensive oil but makes a most luxurious ingredient. You can mix ½ almond oil with ½ safflower oil to reduce expense. If you do this, add 2 drops of Vitamin E which is good for your skin, but is also used as a preservative.

4. Pour the oil into the bottle with the flowers, filling the bottle to the top. Close the bottle with a cork or screw top. Then, if desired, seal the bottle with melted paraffin wax. To do this, first melt the paraffin in a double boiler, adding bits of crayon for coloring if desired. Then dip the sealed bottle upside down several times into the paraffin to coat the top. Turn the bottle right side up, letting the paraffin cool and harden.

Designer: Vicki Baker

12 A Gift of Touch

*W*hen you give someone a massage, you're able to communicate feelings of care and love in a way that transcends words. A massage is a loving gesture you can schedule anytime, it costs almost nothing, and is perhaps the most personal, luxurious, and appreciated gift you can give.

Young and old respond to human touch as a simple expression of caring. Studies show that infants thrive on it and that people live longer and stay healthier when they receive a daily dose of loving hugs.

While massages are beneficial in relieving pain, don't wait until a loved one is suffering before giving them one. If you're unsure where to begin, many good books on a variety of massage techniques are available. Or, just find a bottle of massage oil and follow your tactile instincts.

Massages do not have to be lengthy. Focus on one area such as the hands, or face, or feet. Find a foot reflexology chart to learn the position of pressure points that, when massaged, can contribute to healing and good health.

In selecting a massage oil, choose one made from pure and natural ingredients. You can easily make your own (see page 22) to ensure its freshness and quality. Preparations which contain essential oils distilled from flowers and herbs provide an extra benefit through aroma therapy—the belief that different natural scents can relax or invigorate you.

Beaded Basket of Flowers

13

*C*arol Wilcox Wells created this basket using even-count tubular peyote stitch with a border of chevron chain. The lovely design makes it a perfect keepsake for someone who appreciates the intricacies of the heart as well as of beading.

Designer: Carol Wilcox-Wells

Instructions and Materials are on page 24

MATERIALS

Light switch plate

Rubbing alcohol

Polymer clay—approximately ½ block—of Fimo, Cernit, Premo, or Sculpey III in white

Black and white checkerboard cane

Cornstarch or talcum powder

Small amounts of colored clay for various vegetables

Wax paper

Head pins

TOOLS

Cotton balls

Brayer (small roller), rolling pin, or pasta machine

Cutting blade

Screen, dry sponge, textured leather—anything that will create texture

Needle tool

Small star cutter (optional)

Wood skewers

Round-nose or needle-nose pliers

Vegetable Polymer Light Switch Plate and Fan Pulls

Gardeners and vegetarian cooks will appreciate the humor of the polymer switch plate and fan pulls. They'll know you understand them, having gotten to the root of their passions.

14

Designer: Irene S. Dean

INSTRUCTIONS

If you've never worked with polymer clay, you may want to read Leslie Dierk's book, *Creative Clay Jewelry* (Lark, 1994).

1. Use a small amount of rubbing alcohol on cotton balls to clean the light switch plate, then set aside.

2. First, condition the white clay, then use the brayer, rolling pin, or pasta machine to roll a thin sheet large enough to cover the switch plate. Make it as uniformly thin as possible. Lay this sheet onto the switch plate. Do not trim the clay yet.

3. Using the cutting blade, cut very thin slices from the checkerboard cane. If the slices are too thick, they will distort as you roll, so try to slice the cane as thin as possible.

4. Lay the pieces of cane on the white background in a pleasing arrangement, then roll over them with the brayer or rolling pin to flatten them into the background.

5. Add some texture using a screen, dry sponge, textured leather, or whatever you have available. First, dust the clay with cornstarch or talcum powder so the textured piece won't stick to the clay. Then lay the textured piece on the clay, and, using the brayer or your fingers, press the textured piece into the clay to transfer the pattern. Make sure to press the textured piece onto the edges of the switch plate as well—this will ensure that the clay will adhere. Remove the textured piece and trim any excess clay from the switch plate.

6. Use small amounts of conditioned clay to form the vegetable shapes: **Carrots**—shape orange clay into long tapers, then roll the needle tool across each one to make horizontal ridges. Add feathery bits of green for tops. **Garlic**—for the bulbs, make rounded pieces with pointy tops from off-white clay. Press the needle tool on each, top to bottom, to gently score the bulb. **Broccoli**—make several small round shapes, then roll them together just enough so they stick to one another. Put them on a fat "stalk" that you score with a needle tool. Stipple the broccoli top with an old toothbrush. **Eggplant**—mix a tiny bit of black clay with purple clay, then shape the clay into an elongated egg shape. **Tomatoes**—make orange-red balls. For the eggplant and tomatoes, use the small star cutter to cut leaves for the top from green clay, then press the star shapes onto the tops.

7. Arrange the vegetables on the switch plate. Press gently to adhere to the background. To avoid leaving fingerprints in the vegetables, use a piece of wax paper between the clay shapes and your fingers as you press.

8. Bake the pieces according to the manufacturer's instructions.

9. For vegetable fan pulls, simply shape larger versions of the vegetables as you did in Step 6. Before baking, pierce the centers of the vegetable shapes lengthwise with a needle tool. You may

15 Garden Gifts

Even if you're not a gardener, chances are that someone you love is. One of the best (and almost everlasting) gifts you can give is to plant a tree, flowering shrub, or perennials in another's yard or garden. The symbolism won't be missed. With each new year's growth or flowering, that person will be reminded how the love between you continues to blossom.

In addition to presenting the plant, offer your services for the actual labor. Make sure to provide all information about proper care and feeding. Since avid gardeners rarely leave a nursery without a new plant or two in hand, gift certificates are always appreciated. For something more unusual, find someone to deliver a load of manure or leaf mulch to enrich the soil—a gift only a gardener can love. Your thoughtfulness will be long remembered.

For apartment dwellers, give a window box with plants suitable to that environment. If you know someone who's fortunate enough to have access to a rooftop, a container with patio tomatoes, herbs, a small shrub, or tree can change the skyline to a country vista.

also use a wooden skewer to pierce the shapes, then leave the skewers in while baking the clay. After the pieces are baked and have cooled, thread a gold-colored head pin (used for making beaded jewelry) through the center of each vegetable. Use round-nosed or needle-nosed pliers to wrap the end of the head pin onto a brass ball chain.

Love-Note Cards

*S*imple and elegant, with an unmistakable message, these note cards will get the right idea across to the ones you love. An easy origami fold creates the hearts for these beautiful cards with a three-dimensional look.

17

16 *Say "I Love You!"*

*D*o you say I love you often enough to the people you care about? Every language has an expression that tells in a short phrase that you've given your heart to another. Whether it's Je t'aime (French), Ich liebe dich (German), Te quiero (Spanish), Ti amo (Italian), Ta gra agam ort (Gaelic), Aloha i'a au oe (Hawaiian), Miluji te (Czech), Aishiteru (Japanese), or Ya tyebya lyublyu (Russian), verbalizing these words has a power of its own, mightier than all the other words we own. Saying I love you can be the ultimate expression of love we can give to someone—better than a mountain of gifts, a pile of good intentions, and the promise of a tomorrow that may never come.

MATERIALS

Plain note cards

Decorative papers in several different coordinating patterns

Glue

Foam core, available at craft-supply stores

TOOLS

Scissors

INSTRUCTIONS

1. Cut the background paper from one pattern of decorative paper. Place on the note card in desired position and glue.

2. Cut or fold a heart shape from another pattern of decorative paper. If folding, follow the steps as shown in the illustration.

3. Cut small pieces of foam core. You will use these to raise the hearts for a three-dimensional look.

4. Glue the foam core onto the background paper in the desired positions, then glue the hearts onto the foam core.

5. Cut other pieces of paper into desired shapes and glue onto the background paper. If you prefer, you could raise these with foam core as well.

Tip: When assembling the pieces, do not use too much glue since it can warp the card.

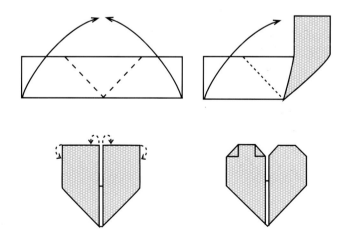

Designer: Pei-Ling Becker

MATERIALS

Old food tin

Enamel spray paint in colors of
your choice

Acrylic paint in colors of your choice

Adhesive-backed paper

Enamel pens

TOOLS

Scissors

Household sponge

INSTRUCTIONS

1. Take the cover off the tin. Using the enamel spray paint, coat the outside of the tin and its cover. To avoid drips, apply two light coats rather than one heavy coat. Allow the first coat to dry thoroughly before applying the second one.

2. Cut shapes from a household sponge. Dip the sponge in acrylic paint until it is evenly covered. Print the design by applying the paint-covered sponges to the tin's surface.

3. Allow the paint to dry, then detail the design with enamel pens.

Variation:

1. Cut shapes of your choice from adhesive-backed paper. After applying the covering coat and allowing it to dry, stick the shapes to the surface of the tin.

2. Using a contrasting color of spray paint, coat the tin. When the paint is dry, carefully peel the adhesive-backed shapes away.

3. Detail the design with enamel pens.

Tip: For a lacy design, use paper lace doilies as stencils. Lay the doilies on a painted tin, then spray a coat of paint over them. Carefully remove the doilies to avoid _smearing the paint. Allow the paint to dry, then detail with enamel pens.

Stenciled Tin

18

Recycle an old food tin by painting it with a fresh design. When you've finished decorating it, fill the tin with cookies, popcorn, or other treats from your kitchen. Once the treats are gone, the tin makes a colorful storage container for toys or craft supplies.

Designer: Ellen Zahorec

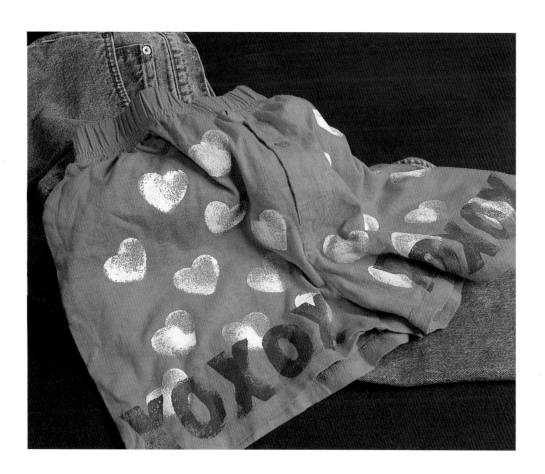

MATERIALS

Cotton, or cotton-
blend boxer shorts in
knit or woven fabric

Newsprint

Fabric paints
or acrylic paint

TOOLS

Scissors

Household sponges

Disposable plate

Stamped Boxers

Forget the silk and lace!
Create practical "romantic"
underwear or sleepwear by stamping
Xs and Os (for kisses and hugs)
on plain boxer shorts. Use the same technique
on an extra-large T-shirt for a
comfortable and lovely night shirt.

19

Designer: Ellen Zahorec

INSTRUCTIONS

1. Using the scissors, cut an X and an O shape from household sponges. You may want to cut several of each in a variety of sizes.

2. Place the newsprint in the middle of the shorts to prevent the paint from soaking through to the other side.

3. Pour the acrylic paint or fabric paint onto the disposable plate.

4. Gently tap the cut sponge into the paint until it is evenly covered.

5. Print the design by applying the paint-covered sponge to the fabric.

6. Some fabric paints need to be heat set. Follow the manufacturer's instructions regarding the method used for setting the dye, as well as for laundering directions.

Dancing Ladies Gourd

Capture the feeling of being in love with this joyful gourd. The design is also a perfect motif for creating a unique gift for a sister or mother.

21

If you've never tried gourd art, this project presents easy instructions for getting started.

MATERIALS

Cured and cleaned gourd, (gourds are available through a local farmers' market— or grow your own!

Water-based black spray enamel

Red, turquoise, and brown permanent markers

Black fine-point felt pen

Clear satin-finish spray lacquer

21, 8-inch (20.5-cm) long pine needles

Brown waxed linen thread

Designer: Dyan Mai Peterson

TOOLS

Stiff scrubbing brush

Pencil

Small power or hand saw

Grapefruit spoon or scraping tool

Coarse- and fine-grit sandpaper

Carbon paper

Wood burning iron

Awl or drill

Embroidery needle

INSTRUCTIONS

The pattern for this design is on page 127.

1. If the outside of the gourd is not clean, use warm water and a stiff brush to remove the dirt and mold. Be careful not to scratch the surface. Allow to dry.

2. Decide which side of the gourd will be the front of the finished piece. With a pencil, draw a line around the top of the gourd; this will become your guide for the top rim. You can make a perfect circle with the help of a compass or draw an abstract, freehand line. You can also choose to leave the gourd whole.

3. On the line at the center back of the gourd, use a small saw to score a starting line for the first cut. Slowly cut back and forth. Now begin to cut all the way around. It will help to point your saw blade in the up and down position.

4. Clean the inside of the gourd using a grapefruit spoon or scraping tool to remove the pulp and seeds.

5. Once the gourd is clean, use a coarse sandpaper on the inside wall, then use a fine-grit sandpaper to further smooth the interior surface. Spray the inside with water-based, black enamel.

6. Copy the pattern on page 127. You may need to enlarge it to fit the size gourd you're using.

7. Place carbon paper under the pattern, then position them on the gourd and trace the design onto the gourd. You may choose to have only one set of the dancing ladies, or you can continue the design all the way around the gourd.

8. Using the wood burning tool, outline the design on the gourd. I chose not to outline the heads and feet and outside arms—although it would look fine if you did.

9. Color in the ladies' dresses using the red and turquoise felt pens. Then color in the heads, arms and feet with a brown felt pen.

10. Add the heart flower bouquets, outlining the hearts with a black fine-point felt pen.

11. At the bottom of the gourd, use the wood burning tool to burn in a wavy line to resemble the ground.

12. Add a few "heart plants" growing from the ground.

13. To seal the gourd and protect your design, apply a fine mist of clear satin-finish spray lacquer. Allow to dry. Apply two to three more coats, allowing each coat to dry thoroughly before applying the next one. Be careful not to use too much lacquer in any one coat, or it will run and create drips.

14. Using the awl or a drill, gently pierce holes ¼" (.5 cm) down from the rim and ½" (1.5 cm) apart all the way around the gourd.

15. With the waxed linen thread, lace the pine needles to the rim of the gourd as shown below.

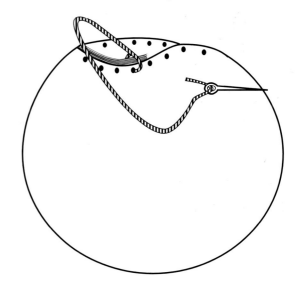

16. Sign and date your work. Happy gourding!

Variations on following page

The Love People

Use the same materials and tools for the dancing ladies gourd, with the addition of a straight edge ruler and an orange permanent marker.

INSTRUCTIONS

1. Follow the same cutting and cleaning process for the dancing ladies gourd.

2. With the ruler and pencil, draw the bodies of the people. This can be great fun. You might choose tall, thin people or short, chubby people—use your creativity!

3. Cut a heart-shaped pattern from a piece of paper. Position the heart shape above each body and trace around it.

4. Using the wood burning tool or a fine-point black marker, burn or draw the arms and hands, legs, feet, and antlers.

5. Use your imagination and have fun designing and coloring the bodies. I used turquoise, orange, red, and brown felt pens.

6. Seal your gourd with clear satin-finish spray lacquer.

7. Lace the pine needles as described in Steps 14 and 15 for the dancing ladies gourd, or leave them off for a more rustic look.

8. Sign and date your work.

The Heart Garden

Use the same materials and tools as for the dancing ladies gourd, with the addition of a gold metallic pen and a green permanent marker.

INSTRUCTIONS

1. Follow the same cutting and cleaning process for the ladies dancing gourd.

2. Make two heart-shaped patterns from a piece of paper—one larger than the other.

3. Randomly place and trace the hearts around the gourd. Color them in with a red permanent marker.

4. Using the wood burning tool or a green permanent marker, add the flower stems in a random and whimsical manner.

5. Use a gold metallic pen to add the swirl design.

6. Seal the gourd with clear satin-finish spray lacquer.

7. Lace the pine needles as described in Steps 14 and 15 for the dancing ladies gourd, or leave them off for a more rustic look.

Memory Boxes

22

Collect memories and give them away. Start with an interesting box or container, or purchase an unpainted box from a craft store and paint and decorate it yourself (designer Terry Taylor used small tins). Inside the box place small mementos that are reminiscent of a special time gone by.

Designer: Terry Taylor

A few small shells, some beach glass, a small gull's feather, and some sand will recapture a beach trip. For a sibling, find replicas of small toys you shared (you may even have kept some of these); an old photo of the house you lived in; pictures of yourselves as children; or an old comic book and baseball cards.

Any item you find that evokes a time and place can go into the box: ticket stubs, play programs, printed napkins, matchbooks, small bits of costume jewelry, military patches, postcards, old letters, or pressed flowers. If you don't have the items on hand, you can have fun searching for them in antique shops or at flea markets and yard sales.

23 *Teacher Gifts*

Do you want to give teachers more than an apple to show how much you appreciate them? Here are a few ideas that may help when you're puzzling about gift ideas at the holidays or the end of the year.

Gift certificates for the classroom are a thoughtful way to give your favorite teachers a gift they can really use. Certificates to an office-supply store allows teachers to go "over budget" to buy classroom extras they might otherwise not be able to afford. A gift certificate to a toy- or art-supply store gives a teacher the means to purchase small items to be used as student incentives for a job well done or admirable behavior. Don't overlook gift certificates to grocery stores so teachers can afford the materials for a classroom cooking project. And, as always, a gift certificate to a bookstore allows a teacher to expand his or her own classroom library.

Ask the teachers if they have a wish list of more expensive items that they might need for the classroom. Then get together with other parents who'll contribute to making that a reality. Whether it's new computer hardware or softwear, videos, chess sets, word games, magazine subscriptions, or donations for a special field trip, you know you're giving your child's teacher a gift that will be well used throughout the year. If you have time, offer to volunteer in the classroom one morning a month.

On a personal note, give teachers a gift certificate for dinner for two to a nice restaurant, a booklet of movie tickets, or a certificate to a specialty store that matches a personal interest. Seasonal gourmet baskets and home-baked goodies are always a treat, as well as paper items such as a box of stationery, a packet of greeting cards, a special pen, or a blank journal.

Salt-Dyed Scarf

*S*ilk scarves are a versatile fashion accessory in any woman's wardrobe. If you've never dyed silk (or any fabric!) this scarf is a great project to get you started. By sprinkling salt on the wet dye, you get a textured effect that looks complicated but is easy to do.

24

MATERIALS

Silk scarf—you can purchase scarves that are already hemmed at art- or craft-supply stores (the scarf shown is 8 x 54" (20.5 x 132 cm)

Canvas stretchers sized to the scarf *

Stainless Steel push pins

Old newspapers

Silk dye resist medium

Silk dye in colors of your choice

Coarse salt

Table salt

* Buy these at art- or craft-supply shops—they're used for stretching canvas for painting. The individual pieces come in a variety of sizes to fit your needs. You can easily assemble the stretchers yourself.

TOOLS

Paintbrushes

Iron

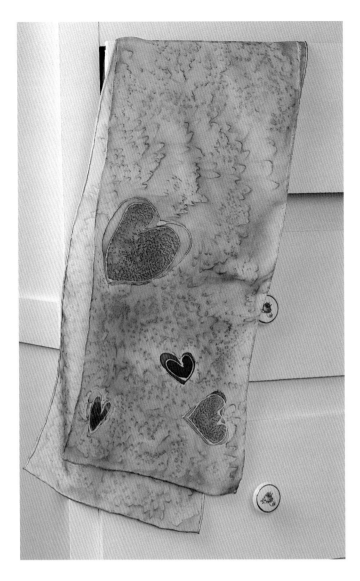

INSTRUCTIONS

1. Assemble the stretcher.

2. Using the stainless steel push pins to pin the rolled edges of the scarf to the wood, carefully stretch the silk scarf on the stretcher. Place the stretcher with the scarf on a floor or table that has been covered with old newspapers.

3. Using the silk dye resist medium, draw the outlines of the hearts. (Imperfect or free-form line drawings make the design more interesting.) Many resists come in disposable containers with applicator tips—otherwise, you may need to paint the resist on with a brush. The resist creates a barrier that prevents the wet dye from getting into (or out of) the area you defined with the resist.

4. Using a paintbrush and following the manufacturer's instructions, apply the dye to the scarf in the area outside the hearts. Start at one edge of the scarf and work toward the opposite edge.

5. Every 12–18" (30.5-45.5 cm), take the coarse salt and carefully sprinkle it on the wet area you've just finished painting. The salt absorbs the moisture, gathering the dye pigments under its grains. You will have little control over the patterning, but will find that the random "blooms" that occur are exciting to watch as they form.

6. Once you've applied salt to the overall surface of the scarf, let the scarf rest for awhile, allowing the salt to gather the moisture. After approximately 25–40 minutes, carefully pour the salt off the scarf. (You can throw the salt away, or dry it and save it for reuse.) Be careful to prevent any splashes of dye or water from getting on the scarf.

7. Apply dye to the areas inside the hearts. While the dye is still wet, apply table salt to those areas. The table salt creates a finer surface design than the larger crystals of the coarse salt.

8. Just as you did for the coarse salt, allow the table salt to remain on the surface for 25–40 minutes, then carefully remove the salt as in Step 6.

9. Allow the scarf to dry thoroughly on the stretcher.

10. When the scarf is dry, follow the dye manufacturer's instructions for heat-setting the dye, either by using a steam iron or baking in the oven.

11. When the dye is set, gently wash out the resist medium and press the scarf with a clean iron (no steam!) that has been set on a wool setting.

12. If the scarf ever looks tired, give it a gentle bath in lukewarm water that has a bit of vinegar added to it.

Designer: Jean Wall Penland

Computer-Generated Gifts

Turn your computer into a love machine! Sophisticated home computers have the capability to produce images that were once only possible to obtain from professional graphic services. Now you can create your own line of personal love notes, stationery, and clothing—all it takes is time and love.

Designer: Susan Kinney

MATERIALS

An original painting, photo, poem, or drawing of you or your loved one

Card stock

Various papers, such as watercolor or handmade papers

T-shirt transfer paper

T-shirts or other fabric items (tote bag, book cover, hat, scarf)

Printer paper

TOOLS

Access to a scanner (your own, a friend's, or a copy shop's)

Computer

Color printer

INSTRUCTIONS

1. Take a favorite "work of art" and scan it; this can be a photo, an original drawing, or a collage that you created from other images. If you don't have a scanner, have a friend scan it, or go to a copy shop, then have them save a copy on a disk. Once you get home, import the scan to your own computer.

2. Use your imagination to play with the image. If you don't like it, "erase" it and start again.

Some techniques to try:

Monotone Print

Take a color print and turn it into a black and white image. Print it on card stock or watercolor paper, then "hand tint" it with pencils or crayons. If you're printing over your painted art work, be careful since water-based paints may make the printer ink run. Print several sizes of the print and experiment with different colors and techniques. This image can then be used as the cover for a handmade card or notebook cover.

Copy, Duplicate, and Design

Multiple images can be arranged and manipulated to be used as headings for notepaper or interesting love-message cards.

Special Papers

Experiment by printing your image in various sizes on special papers. Copies of a painting can be especially effective when printed on glossy card stock or watercolor paper. A photo takes on a very magical look when printed on a handmade paper.

Clothing or Fabric Items

Manipulate the scanned image by changing the colors, stretching the image, duplicating it, or using other interesting artistic variations. Print onto special fabric-transfer paper. Follow the paper manufacturer's directions carefully for applying the transfer. Children love T-shirts and tote bags. A favorite older relative might enjoy a personalized book cover or vest. And the hat lovers in your life would surely appreciate a very special version of printed head wear.

26 Cyber Gifts and Messages

If you have time, a quick e-mail message is a great way to tell someone you're thinking of them. If words fail you, you can easily find web sites on the internet that will download greetings for any occasion to another's computer. Some services offer animated cards with music to accompany the message. Virtual florists offer pictures of lush floral bouquets. You can send postcard images, jokes, and cyber gifts (while not the real item, it's the thought that counts).

Short on time? Forgot a special occasion? Shop from your desk for flowers, candy, jewelry, and perfume by tapping the internet for an array of gift-giving opportunities. On-line shopping services offer everything from books to art, car parts to luxury trips, sporting goods to ballet tickets.

27 Lunch-Box Notes

Keep your love alive! Let them know you're thinking about them throughout the day. It only takes a moment, even on the busiest mornings, to write a short message and slip it in a lunch box or brown bag. Keep pads of small self-adhesive note paper handy for this purpose. For children, vary your messages from humorous to encouraging; for a spouse, serious to saucy.

Don't underestimate the power of a good note. Knowing that someone out there cares about you can transform a bad morning into a great day. If you happen to skip a few days without notes, your family will let you know—a good indication of how much they enjoy your words of love.

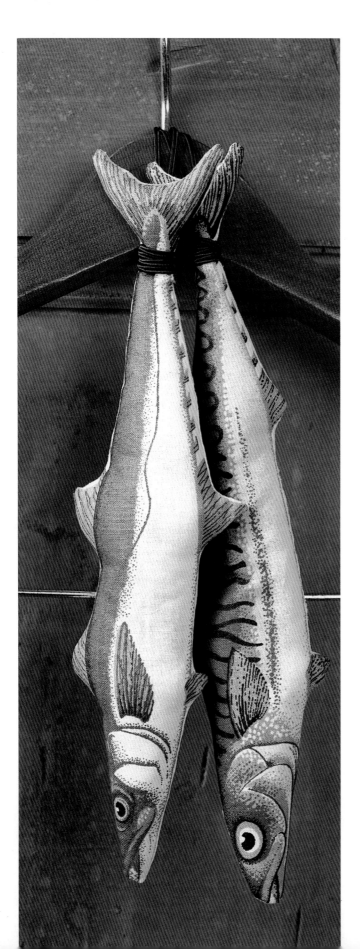

Print-Fabric Sachet

Find theme fabrics with large motifs that match a man's hobby or interests, then turn it into a hanging sachet. Many home-decorating fabrics feature prints with cars, boats, and sports images.

MATERIALS

Print fabric

Solid fabric for backing

Polyester pillow fill

Scent pellets

Narrow soutache cord

TOOLS

Scissors

Needle and thread

INSTRUCTIONS

1. Select a printed fabric. The outline of the individual images should be fairly simple.

2. For your cutting line, measure ⅜" (1 cm) away from the outer edge of the image. With a pencil, draw all the way around the image at this measurement.

3. Cut the image out along the cutting line.

4. Lay the cut-out image on the backing fabric, right sides together. Trace the image on the backing fabric, then cut it out.

5. Place the image and the backing right sides together, and using a ⅜" (1 cm) seam allowance, sew along the edges. Leave a small opening to turn the sachet right side out.

6. Clip the curves and trim the seam allowance to ¼" (.5 cm). Turn the sachet right side out.

7. Stuff with polyester filling.

8. Using the scissor blade, make a slit in the center of the stuffing to create a small pocket for the scent pellets. Insert the scent pellets into this pocket.

9. Fold the seam allowance in on the opening and slip stitch closed.

10. Cut a length of soutache, approximately 6" (15 cm) long. Leaving a ¼" (.5 cm) tail, sew one end of the soutache at the point where you want the hanging loop.

11. Make a 2" (5 cm) loop with the soutache. At the point where you attached the soutache in Step 10, secure the end of the loop with a few stitches.

12. Wrap the remaining soutache around the base of the loop (in this design, the end is wrapped around the fish tails). Tuck the small remaining end of the soutache under the wrapped area and secure it with a few stitches.

Designer: Lisa Sanders

Snowflake-Swirl Baby Bonnet

29

You don't have to be a grandmother to make this classic baby bonnet. Aunts, godmothers, and friends will also find it a great project to knit for welcoming a new member to the family, community, or neighborhood. To create an heirloom treasure, make it in white for a christening.

MATERIALS

1-¾ oz. (50 g) = 192 yds (173 m) machine-washable baby weight yarn (Baby Ull by Dale, Deep Yellow #2015).

24" (60 cm) of ribbon

TOOLS

Knitting needles, size 3 U.S. (3.25 mm)

Crochet hook, size C/2 (2.75 mm, 3 mm)

INSTRUCTIONS

Size: Baby's size seven to nine months

Gauge: Over Snowflake Pattern, 7 sts = 1" (2.5 cm)

Designer: Charlene Schurch

Finished measurement: 14" (35 cm) around the face, 6" (15 cm) from crown to face.

1. Cast on 9 sts. **Row 1:** Knit. **Row 2, 4, 6, 8, 10, 12, 14:** Purl. **Row 3:** K1, (*yo, k1* repeat to last st) k1. **Row 5:** K1, (*yo, k2* repeat to last st) k1. **Row 7:** K1, (*yo, k3* repeat to last st) k1. **Row 9:** K1, (*yo, k1, yo, k1, k2tog* repeat to last st) k1. **Row 11:** K1, (*yo, k1, yo, k2, k2tog* repeat to last st) k1. **Row 13:** K1, (*yo, k1, yo, k3, k2tog* repeat to last st) k1. **Row 15:** K1, (*yo, k1, yo, k2, yo, k2, k2tog* repeat to last st) k1. **Row 16:** P1, (*p2tog, p7* repeat to last st) p1. **Row 17:** K1, (*yo, k1, yo, k2, yo, k3, k2tog* repeat to last st) k1. **Row 18:** P1, (*p2tog, p8* repeat to last st) p1. **Row 19:** K1, (*yo, k1, yo, k2, yo, k4, k2tog* repeat to last st) k1. **Row 20:** P1, (*p2tog, p9* repeat to last st) p1. **Row 21:** K1, (*yo, k1, yo, k2, yo, k5, k2tog* repeat to last st) k1. **Row 22:** P1, (*p2tog, p10* repeat to last st) p1. **Row 23:** K1, (*yo, k1, yo, k2, yo, k6, k2tog* repeat to last st) k1. **Row 24:** P1, (*p2tog, p11* repeat to last st) p1. **Row 25:** K1, (*yo, k1, yo, k2, yo, k7, k2tog* repeat to last st) k1. **Row 26:** P1, (*p2tog, p12* repeat to last st) p1. (93 sts in all).

2. For the bonnet sides, knit one row, increasing 2 stitches evenly as you work across (95 sts).

3. *Snowflake Pattern:* Work back and forth in the pattern for approx 4" (10 cm) ending with pattern row 1 or 7 (a purl row after a complete snowflake).

Row 1, 3, 5, 7, 9, 11: K1 in the back of the st. *Purl all sts to last one* slip last stitch with yarn in front (sl 1 wyif). **Row 2:** K1-B (k4 *ssk, yo, k1, yo, k2tog, k3; rep from *, end k1) sl 1 wyif. **Row 4:** K1-B (k5 *yo, sl 2-k 1-p2so, yo, k5; rep from *) sl 1 wyif. **Row 6:** Repeat Row 2. **Row 8:** K1-B (ssk, yo, k1, yo, k2tog, *k3, ssk, yo, k1, yo, k2 tog; rep from *) sl 1 wyif. **Row 10:** K1-B (k1, *yo, sl 2-k 1-p2so, yo, k5; rep from *, end last repeat k1) sl 1 wyif. **Row 12:** Repeat Row 8.

4. Work 4 rows of stockinette stitch (knit right-side rows and purl wrong-side rows). Work eyelet row: K1, *k2tog, yo* continue working across to last 2 sts, k1, sl 1 wyif. Work 4 more rows of stockinette stitch. Bind off loosely.

5. To finish, sew the swirl pattern together and run the yarn through the 9 cast-on sts and draw up tightly. Darn in other ends. Turn hem to wrong side along eyelet row and sew in place. Single crochet (sc) in every row along bottom edge of the bottom. SC one more row. Sew a 12" (30 cm) piece of ribbon to each front corner of the bonnet. Block gently to shape.

Abbreviations

k1-b	knit one stitch in the back loop
k2tog	knit two together
p2tog	purl two together
sc	single crochet
sl 1	slip one as if to purl
sl 2-k1-p2so	slip two, knit one, pass two slipped stitches together over the knit stitch (vertical double decrease)
ssk	slip, slip, knit
st(s)	stitch(es)
wyif	with yarn in front
yo	yarn over

MATERIALS

15-bean mix

Decorative glass jar or container

Flavor packet—spices, herbs, and bouillon flavor of your choice

Optional: fresh vegetables, a favorite sausage, homemade vegetable stock, wooden spoon, soup cups

INSTRUCTIONS

1. Place the 15-bean mixture in an interesting glass jar. You may be able to buy beans already mixed, or, have fun exploring the markets to find as many varieties as you can.

2. Create a seasoning packet by mixing spices and herbs and placing them in a small envelope or plastic bag. Include powdered bouillon for an instant soup base. Place the small bag on top of the beans in the jar.

3. Copy these basic instructions:

   Soak the beans for approximately nine hours (overnight is best). Discard the soaking water and rinse the beans. Place the beans in a soup pot and cover with fresh, cold water. Add the contents of the flavor packet.

   Cook the beans all day over very low heat on the stove, or follow the directions for cooking beans in an electric slow cooker.

   For the last two hours of cooking, add fresh vegetables, and/or sausage.

Tip: For a deluxe presentation, include a jar of your homemade soup base, fresh vegetables, and/or sausage, then add a wooden spoon for stirring, and two oversized soup cups for serving.

15-Bean Soup Mix

30

Assembling recipe ingredients can be fun when you know you're giving them away! Grandmothers and soup lovers of all ages will enjoy this special treat. Don't be surprised if your family and friends wait awhile to make the soup—the variety of beans used in this mix makes a colorful and interesting kitchen decoration.

Designer: Traci Dee Neil-Taylor

31 Plan a Special Meal

It's natural to think of music or poetry as the soul of love. But when it comes to a meal that's been thoughtfully and lovingly prepared, good food dictates amorous messages to the heart swifter than a melodious chord or a well-turned metaphor.

The ultimate luxury is to serve someone you love breakfast in bed. Add the morning paper or a favorite magazine to the presentation, and it's an invitation to stretch a glorious hour into a luxurious, languid morning of pampering.

Fresh flowers and garnishes added to the tray and plates provide extra color and highlights. Whatever you make, make it fresh. Scones, muffins, waffles— all are easy to make, even for those who don't usually cook. You may want to consider incorporating edible flowers (see page 70) into your recipe.

Create a surprise for other meals, such as an impromptu picnic at the park in the middle of the day or in front of the fire after work. Put together a make-ahead casserole, bring it over to a friend's, pop it in the oven, and catch up on the gossip while it's cooking. Pick a country, find recipes from it, gather the ingredients and cook it together. Establish a dish or dessert that's only served when a loved one is celebrating a special occasion, such as the end of a large project, a child's great grades, or a new job.

Investigate aphrodisiacs. Artichokes, asparagus, oysters, tomatoes, strawberries, and chocolate are only a few of the foods said to enhance feelings of love. While there may be some truth to this based on a food's chemical composition, the real element that stimulates amorous notions may be the thoughts of love and seduction you put into creating a feast for the one you love.

Polymer Clay Pins, Tie Tacks, and Earrings

32

Even if you've never worked with polymer clay, you can easily make "lovely" little pins, earrings, and tie tacks. For a novel presentation, attach the finished pieces of small jewelry to interesting cards made from decorative papers.

Designer: Susan Kinney

MATERIALS

Polymer clay in various colors

Gilding cream or gold leaf

Clear spray varnish

Jewelry findings as needed—tie tacks, earring wires or backs, pin backs

Strong, quick-drying glue (cyanoacrylate glue works best with polymer clay)

TOOLS

Pencil or pointed tool

Conventional oven or toaster oven used in a well-ventilated room

Aluminum foil or baking sheet

Textured surface (wallpaper, stone, tile, etc.)

INSTRUCTIONS

Heart Jewelry

1. Condition a small piece of clay that is appropriate to the size heart you wish to make. You can do this by warming the clay in your hands for a few minutes before kneading it until it is easily

pliable. You can also tuck the clay into a small plastic bag and put the bag in your pocket, allowing the clay to warm while you do other tasks, then knead when ready.

2. Shape the conditioned clay into a ball. On a covered surface, press down onto the clay to flatten. Using your fingers, shape it into a heart. You may need to use a pointed tool or pencil to help you in the shaping. It doesn't have to be perfect—and may be more interesting and artistic if you experiment with the shape.

3. Lay the clay on a flat, smooth piece of aluminum foil, or on a baking sheet. Bake the clay, following the manufacturer's instructions.

4. Cool completely, then gild, using either the gilding cream or gold leaf, following the product directions.

5. In a well-ventilated area, or outside, spray with the clear varnish to seal.

6. Apply jewelry findings with glue.

7. If desired, make a special card and attach the gift.

Variations

Cane Heart

Cut a simple clay cane into a heart shape and surround or embed it with solid-color polymer clay. These can be used in multiples, or as a single heart, for an interesting piece of jewelry.

Initial Jewelry

Condition the polymer clay and roll it into a tube shape. Form the tube into a loved one's initial, or experiment with creating an entire name or word. Gently press the initial or name into an interesting textured surface to transfer the pattern to the clay. Bake according to the manufacturer's instructions. When cool, gently rub the textured surface with gilding cream and buff. Seal with the clear spray varnish and attach appropriate jewelry findings.

Doggie Biscuits

Don't forget your best friend when giving a gift of love! Create a homemade treat from your own kitchen for your dog, a neighborhood pal, or a friend's pampered pet. There are no unpronounceable mystery ingredients in this recipe—just wholesome food to keep your loving pet healthy and strong.

Designer: Traci Dee Neil-Taylor

INGREDIENTS

1½ cups whole wheat flour

½ cup powdered milk

1 tsp. salt

1 tsp. sugar

1 egg

Water

The yield depends on the size of cookie cutter you use. Look for a novelty cookie cutter in a kitchen store—these biscuits were made with a cutter shaped like a bone.

1. Preheat the oven to 350°F (175°C).

2. In a large bowl, mix the dry ingredients together. Beat the egg, then stir into the dry ingredients.

3. Add the water gradually, using just enough to make the dough moist and to hold it together.

4. Turn the dough onto a surface that has been lightly floured with additional whole wheat flour. Using a rolling pin, roll the dough out and cut with a cookie cutter.

5. Bake in the preheated oven for 10–15 minutes or until golden brown.

6. Let the biscuits cool thoroughly before giving to your pet.

34 Pet Gifts

Most of us don't need any prompting when it comes to spoiling our pets. Because they give us so much unconditional love, we, in turn, want to occasionally show them extra measures of our love with a special treat or gift.

Dogs love chew toys, balls for fetching, or ropes for tugging. Try the recipe for homemade dog biscuits. Look for herbal shampoos, a new collar and leash, or a colorful sweater. Select healthy treats, design and build a dog palace, or get your older dog a comfortable bed.

Satisfy your cat's pouncing nature with catnip mice, balls, and toys that squeak. Elaborate structures for cats can be fun to design and construct. Include columns covered in old carpet scraps for scratching and a cushioned ledge for lounging. Make the dancing cats needlepoint frame (see page 111) to hold a special picture of your fancy feline.

More than the toys and trinkets we give them, pets appreciate the gift of our undivided attention: an extra 15 minutes added to a walk, moments spent luxuriating in our laps, and a few extra pats or a scratch here and there.

MATERIALS

Box with lid,
approximately 9 x 9"
(23 x 23 cm)

Decorative paper

White craft glue

TOOLS

Scissors

Paintbrush

Pencil

Craft knife with a disposable
blade or a utility knife

Treasure Box

Make this treasure box for a child,
special friend, or partner. Fill the box
with small gifts for every day of one
week, or every month of one year. (If
you're feeling particularly loving and generous,
use an extra large box and fill it with a gift
for every day of the year!) Thinking of
presents that are especially tailored to
an individual is challenging and fun.

35

Designer: Laura Sims

INSTRUCTIONS

Box

1. Cut a 4" (10 cm) square hole in the center of the box lid.

2. Put the lid on the box.

3. Measure the length and width of the top of the box. Measure the depth of the side. To determine the correct size for the covering, first add the length measurement to the depth measurement of 2 sides, then add an additional inch (2.5 cm) for each side. Next, add the width measurement to the depth measurement of 2 sides, then add an additional inch (2.5 cm) for each side.

4. Cut a piece of the decorative paper to the size you determined in Step 3.

5. On a separate piece of decorative paper, trace around the lid, then cut this shape out.

6. Using the small brush and craft glue, brush the glue on the lid of the closed box. Center the paper cut in Step 5 on the lid and press to adhere.

7. Follow the instructions for covering a square box on pages 116–117 with this exception: adhere the 1" (2.5 cm) surplus to the base of the box, then brush glue on the traced shape and adhere it to the base of the box.

8. After covering the box, turn it over so the lidded top faces up. With your fingers, find the four corners of the 4" (10 cm) cut square and mark the points with a pencil. Using the knife, cut a diagonal cross in the square from corner to corner. Brush glue on the underside of the four sections and adhere them to the underside of the lid.

Gift Ideas

1. Make certificates by cutting small rectangles of paper, then write your desired message on them. Roll them up and tie them with a ribbon. Message ideas may be: a quote; an invitation for dinner, a camping trip, or a long walk; a promise; a secret; or a service.

2. Find miniature objects such as small bottles of bubble bath or small cakes of soap, two candles for an evening alone at home, a spool of thread to hem one pair of slacks, a special book, or a bottle of heart and star stickers or confetti.

3. Jewelry.

4. Objects found in nature of significance to that person.

36 Tell a Story

Don't let distance stand in your way—create your own story tapes for faraway grandchildren! You can stay close by reading them a nightly bedtime story, even though it may be months until your next visit. Simply select a book, then record yourself reading it aloud. Send the tape and book to a grandchild, and they can enjoy your company even though you're miles apart.

On one side of the tape, record the story without interruption. On the other side of the tape, explain that you'll ring a bell when it's time to turn the page. Very young children will enjoy snuggling with Mom or Dad who'll turn the pages for them as they listen to the uninterrupted story. As they get older, aspiring readers will enjoy the other side of the tape. They'll feel very grown up when they can turn the pages by themselves, following along as you read.

For variety, try your hand at creating your own simple book, based on stories from your own childhood or from pure flights of fancy. Draw simple pictures or use old family photographs to illustrate your text.

When grandchildren outgrow storybooks, record your own stories on tape that include recollections and remembrances from when you were young, your travels, your experiences, and anecdotes about friends and relatives. While staying in touch with those you love, you'll also be preserving family history for future generations.

1. Play with the tiles and beads, arranging them into a pleasing, symmetrical design. Different shapes and sizes of beads can be used. The gold, green, and red beads used in this design were chosen to complement the colors in the tiles.

2. Fit the drill or craft tool with a small bit (or one suited to the size of the pieces to be drilled). Drill holes in the tiles from side to side. (Depending on the pieces in your design, you may need to drill the holes from top to bottom.)

3. Using the needle and beading string, string the beads and tiles. When all the beads and tiles are strung, tie the ends of the string together. For extra security, begin with a doubled length of string and secure the ends with two or more square knots.

4. When the ends have been tied, return the ends back through the beads to hide the string—one end in each direction.

Mah-Jongg Tile Necklace

37

If you can drill a hole, you can make a necklace! Adapt this design by using a variety of old game pieces, such as dominoes, cribbage pieces, or dice—all of which you can find in antique shops. This could also be an interesting project made with golf tees.

Designer: Nancy McGaha

MATERIALS

Mah-jongg tiles (the ones used are "flowers")

Beads to complement tile colors

TOOLS

Drill or craft tool and small bit

Beading string

Needle

38 # Donate to Charity

Some people claim they have everything they need, making it very difficult when you want to express your love for them with a gift. If you can't overcome your urge to give, don't waste those feelings of generosity—instead make a charitable donation to an organization, non-profit group, or church in that person's name.

Select a charity you've heard the person mention or find one that matches a cause the honoree supports. If you don't know what group they favor, give them a certificate that states you will donate a designated amount to a charity of their choice in their name.

Make volunteering a gift. Offer to donate time to another's favorite organization. While some non-profit and charitable groups appreciate only monetary gifts, many need to fill schedules with volunteer hours to accomplish their work.

2. Cut the candle wicking approximately ½" (1.5 cm) longer than the length of the cut beeswax sheet.

3. Lay the wicking on the beeswax sheet lengthwise, close to one of the long edges. One end of the wicking should be flush to the bottom edge of the sheet; the other end should extend to create the wick.

4. At the edge with the wicking, begin to roll the beeswax. Make sure the wick is straight and in the center of the roll. Apply an even, gentle pressure as you roll the wax sheet. Do not press too hard; it may deform the candle.

5. Trim the end of the wick to ¼" (.5 cm).

6. If you're giving these as gifts, make a simple wrapper from corrugated cardboard and tie with a ribbon or raffia.

Designer: Traci Dee Neil-Taylor

Rolled Beeswax Candles

39

There's nothing more romantic than candlelight—if you remembered to pick up the candles. Don't let a loving evening slip by in darkness. Keep a few sheets of beeswax on hand, and you'll be only seconds away from setting the mood.

MATERIALS

Sheets of "honeycomb" beeswax, available at craft-supply stores

Candle wicking

TOOLS

Craft knife

Scissors

INSTRUCTIONS

1. Using the craft knife, cut the sheet of beeswax according to the size candle you want—tall or short, thick or thin.

40 *Make Time*

When asked, most people wish for the gift of time to accomplish all they need to do. While it's not within our power to stretch twenty-four hours into twenty-six (or -seven or -eight), we can give others the gift of time when we offer to do time-consuming chores as our gift to them.

Raking leaves, cleaning a basement or garage, painting, washing a car, pulling weeds, washing windows, doing laundry, walking the dog, grocery shopping, cooking a meal, running errands, and babysitting, are some examples of ways you can "buy" precious time for busy loved ones.

One way to present this gift is through a coupon booklet. Create coupons redeemable for the indicated chores, staple them together, and slip them into an envelope or tuck them in a card. The recipient can redeem the coupons for your services when needed. On page 125, you'll find a coupon you can copy with blank spaces you can fill in accordingly.

Pressed-Flower Magnets

Don't hide your love! These floral magnets are particularly appropriate when you want to leave someone a flowery love note that can't be missed.

MATERIALS

Glass cleaner

2" (5 cm) square of glass *

Pressed flowers and leaves (see page 79)

White glue

2" (5 cm) square of beveled glass *

⅜" (1 cm) copper or silver foil tape *

½" (1.5 cm) heavy-duty button magnet

* If you can't find the small plain and beveled glass or the foil tape at a craft-supply store, you'll be able to find them through stained-glass suppliers.

TOOLS

Toothpicks

Scissors

Orange stick

INSTRUCTIONS

1. With the glass cleaner, clean the 2" (5 cm) square of glass, and arrange two to five thin flowers and leaves on it. If you're layering the flowers and leaves, keep your layer as thin as possible.

2. Gently lift the edges of the flowers with a toothpick, and apply a tiny dot of white glue on the back of the flower at its stem or thicker portion so that the glue won't show through. Allow to dry.

3. Using the glass cleaner, gently clean around the design, then clean the beveled square of glass.

4. Place the beveled glass on the glass with the design, lining up the edges of both pieces of glass so they're even. Gently squeeze the two pieces together as you begin to lay the foil tape along the edges. Start ⅛" (.3 cm) away from one corner and continue around the square. As you work, keep the tape's width centered between the two pieces of glass. When you've gone completely around the square, cut the foil tape with scissors.

5. Press the foil tape onto the front of the glass. When you get to the corners, tuck the folds into the corners as you press along each side. Do the same with the back. Finish by burnishing (rubbing) the foil flat and smooth with an orange stick or the back of your fingernail.

6. Glue a small, heavy-duty magnet to the back where it won't show through. Allow time to dry, then clean the glass again.

Tip: The colors of the flowers will last longer if you keep the magnets out of direct sunlight.

Designer: Cheri Hoefelmeyer

Desk Accessories

ake one, or all, of these accessories to decorate the desk space of a hard-working loved one. The designs will lend an artistic flair to even the most mundane tasks.

42-44

The large box and small stamp dispenser, letter openers, and pen and holder are all embellished with polymer clay. Designer Sheila Sheppard says you can easily adapt the technique for other projects, such as an inlaid photo frame, or for recycling by giving new life to old objects.

Designer: Sheila A. Sheppard

Inlaid Boxes

MATERIALS

Unfinished, pine craft boxes: large 3 x 5" (7.5 x 12.5 cm); small 2 x 4" (5 x 10 cm)

One block black polymer clay

Partial blocks or scraps of polymer clay in assorted colors

Assorted, preformed, polymer clay canes, available at craft stores— or make your own

1 sheet metallic leaf in gold and blue multi-color

Gold metallic powder

Medium-grit sandpaper

Acrylic paint in teal, or color of your choice—you may prefer using wood stain for coloring the box

TOOLS

Craft knife

Pencil

Emery board

Rolling pin or pasta machine

Metal ruler

Slicing blade

Skewer or needle tool

Oven

Large glass baking dish

Oven parchment

Toothpicks

Medium-bristle paint brush

Paper towels

Clean rag

INSTRUCTIONS

If you've never worked with polymer clay, you may want to read Leslie Dierk's book, *Creative Clay Jewelry* (Lark, 1994).

1. Using the craft knife, gently scratch a "toothy" surface on the box wherever you will be applying the polymer clay. This lets the wood receive the clay so it will bond well when baked. (Because this box has recessed panels, the scratches were made inside the recesses.) Clean debris away.

2. For the small stamp box, make a slot for the stamps. Use a pencil to mark the box on the upper inside of one of the small ends. Draw a small rectangle ⅛" (.3 cm) wide and slightly longer than the stamps. With the craft knife, score along the outline of the rectangle several times, firmly but gently, until you cut through wood. Remove the rectangle and sand the surfaces smooth with an emery board.

3. For the small stamp box, use a rolling pin or pasta machine to roll some of the black polymer clay into a thin sheet that is large enough to cover the areas you've chosen. *NOTE: Use separate utensils for working with polymer clay. Do not use kitchen utensils that are used for food preparation.*

4. Take the foil leaf and lay it over the clay sheets. Roll gently until the foil adheres to the clay—just enough to give the clay an antiqued, crackled effect.

5. Using the ruler, measure the areas on the box that you want to cover with the clay. Cut the clay sheets with foil accordingly to size.

6. Lay the pieces on the pre-scratched surfaces of the box and press gently. Repeat all around. (The small box in the photo was covered on the bottom and inside, but this is optional.) You may cover the top as you did the other surfaces, or save it for last to create a more fancy inlay.

7. For a fancier top experiment with your own designs—they can be as complex as your skill and imagination allow. The following instructions detail the design for each box.

For the stamp box: Make a thicker foiled slab by adding more clay under one of the thinner sheets made in Steps 3 and 4. Cut the slab to fit the area of the top of the box to be covered. Place and press

INSTRUCTIONS

Pen

1. Remove the top cap from the pen. Using the needle-nose pliers, grasp the tapered metal shaft of the pen (just above the writing tip) and pull straight out—set both pieces aside.

2. Roll one-half of the block of black clay until it is ¹⁄₁₆" (.16 cm) thick or less. If you're using a pasta machine, set it at the highest setting. From this sheet, cut a piece that is 1¼ x 6" (3 x 15 cm).

3. Using the steel wool, roughen the white pen sheath, then dust.

4. Lay the pen sheath lengthwise onto the sheet of black clay. Cover the sheath with the clay sheet, trimming off any excess clay. Smooth the surface. If there are any bubbles, use the needle tool to pierce them, then smooth the clay.

5. Take the gold leaf and lay it over the remaining sheet of black clay. Roll gently until the leaf adheres to the clay—just enough to give the clay an antiqued, crackled effect.

6. Cut out several ¹⁄₁₆" (.16 cm) wide strips from this sheet, then set the rest aside. Take the clay-covered pen sheath, and, starting at the tip end, begin wrapping these strips around it (refer to photo). Keep adding strips until you get to the top, then gently twist the clay.

7. Take the gold-leafed clay sheet, and, using the small star cutter, or a cutter in the shape of your choice, cut the shapes and add them to top of the pen. Set the remaining sheet of clay aside.

8. Apply a small amount of gold and green metallic powders to the shapes on the top (and the pen sheath, if desired), and rub in gently for an antiqued look.

9. Preheat the oven to 275°F (135°C). Lay the pen in the baking dish lined with parchment and bake for 30 minutes. Insert the ink shaft with pen tip, which you removed in Step 1, into the clay sheath.

Pen Holder

1. With the 3½" long x 1½" wide x 1" high (9 x 4 x 2.5 cm) block of leftover clay scraps, shape a slight taper at one end.

2. Roll one-half of the block of black clay until it is ¹⁄₁₆" (.16 cm) thick or less. If you're using a pasta machine, set it at the highest setting. From this sheet, cut a 6 x 5" (15 x 12.5 cm) piece. Wrap this piece lengthwise around the block made in Step 1 (like wrapping a gift). Trim the excess and smooth neatly. Cut two gold-leafed clay strips from the sheet made for the pen, and apply to top and sides of the block.

3. Emboss the block by pressing the wire screen, net fabric, or lace into the top of the block, slightly overlapping the sides. Remove and apply metallic powders lightly to the surface to highlight the design.

4. Take the copper wire and measure 1½" (4 cm) from one end. Bend the wire down at this point. At the end of this bent piece, use the needle-nose pliers to make a rounded curve. Lay the bent and curved end of the wire on the anvil, then flatten with the rubber mallet.

5. At the other end of the wire, mark a point 1" (2.5 cm) from the end. Above that point, coil the wire around the tapered metal dowel (working from the tapered end up) until you get to the flattened section. Below the 1" (2.5 cm) mark, use the pliers to make an angular zigzag.

6. To hold the pen, you want the coiled wire to slant approximately 45° from the top of the block, with the hammered coil pointing down toward the block. Hold the wire in this position and insert the 1" (2.5 cm) zigzag of wire into the prepared block approximately ¼" (.5 cm) from the inside of the gold-leafed strip that is closest to the wide end of the block. Gently press in around hole. To anchor the wire, make a pea-sized square of black clay and push it into the block around the copper coil.

7. Preheat the oven to 275°F (135°C). Lay the block in the glass baking dish lined with parchment paper. Bake for one hour. Allow to cool completely.

8. Insert the pen into the coil to complete the set.

Collage Cards

Have fun making these unique cards, then send them whenever you want to highlight a special greeting or love note

45

MATERIALS

Decorative papers

White craft glue

Blank greeting cards and envelopes— or make your own

Heart-shaped sequins

TOOLS

Scissors—straight and/or decorative edge

Heart-shaped hole punch

Small brush

INSTRUCTIONS

The pattern for the decorative envelope is on page 129.

1. Select decorative papers.

2. Choose a quilt pattern you like. Cut geometric shapes from the papers and piece them together, using your quilt pattern as inspiration, then glue. Accent the card with heart-shaped sequins or hearts made with the heart-shaped hole punch.

3. Make a small envelope (see pattern on page 129), or use a pre-made one. Take an old card or reproduction and cut out the desired area. Partially insert the motif in the envelope and glue it into that position. Accent the design with sequins and hearts. Write your message on the blank side of the envelope.

Tip: With collage, you're only limited by your imagination—make your card as plain or as fancy as you desire. Investigate using decorative-edge scissors for adding an interesting touch to the collage pieces, the card edges, or envelope.

Designer: Laura Sims

MATERIALS

Small lamp with a white or pale-color shade

Tracing paper

Acrylic paint

TOOLS

Pencil

Brush

INSTRUCTIONS

1. Remove the shade.

2. Draw the design directly on the shade. Or, if you prefer, create a design and copy it onto tracing paper. Turn the tracing paper over and trace over the lines of the design. Lay the paper on the shade and, once more, trace over the lines to transfer the design to the shade's surface.

3. Paint the design. Do not thin the paint too much as you work because the paint will become watery and bleed through the shade.

4. Attach the shade, turn the lamp on, and admire your work!

49 Share Your Talents

Can you play a concerto, know how to tango, or sew like a pro? Do you know how to knit or crochet? Can you refinish furniture or build a bookcase? Are you handy at wallpapering, know how to bead, or build model ships? Do you feel comfortable under the hood of a car, love Italian cooking, or know how to center a pot? Whatever your skills and talents, sharing them with others is one of the greatest gifts you can give.

Present a certificate to a loved one that's good for five, 10 or 50 lessons, however many you want to give. In that time, work together to produce an item or meet a goal. Young and old alike will appreciate the one-on-one attention you give them. As you and your pupil progress, you'll both share a sense of accomplishment that money can't buy.

Switched-On Hearts

Turn on a love light! This decorated switch plate will remind someone special that your love can light up even their darkest night.

50

MATERIALS

Cardboard

Decorative papers

Heavyweight paper

Acrylic gloss medium

Dimensional paint

Switch plate

Clear silicone sealant

TOOLS

Scissors

Craft knife

Old newspapers or wax paper

1"(2.5 cm) paintbrush

Nail or piercing tool

INSTRUCTIONS

Patterns for this design are on page 130.

1. Copy the patterns for this design onto the cardboard and cut out. Feel free to create your own design by making different patterns of your choice.

2. Using the cardboard shapes, trace the outlines of the medium and small heart, two flowers, and the rectangular background (or use patterns of your own design) onto the decorative papers. Cut them out. Using the same cardboard shapes, trace them onto the heavyweight paper and cut out.

3. Glue the decorative-paper shapes to the heavyweight paper shapes. When dry, use a craft knife to cut out a center rectangle for the switch from the larger rectangular piece.

4. Position the pieces on the rectangular background as shown in the photo, or use an alternative arrangement. Make sure to keep the hole for the switch in the center of the design free from any obstruction.

5. Lay the piece on old newspapers or wax paper, and brush a coating of gloss medium on the front of the piece. Let this dry thoroughly, checking as it dries so it won't stick to the newspaper or wax paper. Apply a second coat, and allow to dry thoroughly.

6. With dimensional paint, outline and decorate your switch plate. When dry, glue the work to the purchased switch plate using a silicone sealant. Let dry.

7. Use a nail or piercing tool to poke holes through the paper for the plate screws.

51 *Make a Mix Tape*

Music will always be a powerful force in the lives of lovers. Many couples have a song they claim as their own. Often significant events, such as a first date, an engagement, even a breakup, are remembered by the music that was playing at the time. The right lyrics, melody, and artist can often express your thoughts and emotions to those you love better than you can using your own words and sentiments.

Home recording capabilities allow you to make a tape that's a mix of many tracks from many different sources. You can record from compact discs, other tapes, even vinyl records if you still have them. The actual recording is easy but time-consuming. You need to stay with it, monitoring each segment so there is a smooth, clean transition between tracks.

While making a good mix tape is easy, making a great mix tape—one that's a memorable expression of your love—is an art. Don't take the thought process behind creating a tape too lightly. The cuts you finally select will be as individualistic as your handwriting—after all, you're customizing your sentiments.

Use a variety of different musical styles for an effective tape. Mix mellow jazz with rhythm and blues, add a hint of pop, then some vintage rock. Make a tape of love arias from operas you've listened to or attended together. Find songs from the countries you've visited, music that recaptures your trip. Try adding a funny song from childhood—this provides a nice transition between moods. A string of country and western songs, thoughtfully placed, can tell the whole story (and then some) of your relationship.

Listening to a great mix can be an emotional experience, causing tears, a smile, even outright laughter. Many long-distance relationships have been kept alive by spanning the gap with audio tape. Just remember, no matter what music you choose, or how you assemble it, a great mix should always, always leave the listener thinking of you.

Calendula Soap

Making soap is easier than you think. With a little care and caution you can make this very personal gift. The recipe uses calendula flowers, almond oil, and lemon grass essential oil to give the soap a sunny scent—but you can substitute other botanicals and oils to the likings of your love.

52

INGREDIENTS

Yield: 42, 4 oz. (112 g) bars

6 cups (1.5 L) cold distilled or spring water

1⅓ cans (473 grams) 100% lye

44 oz. (.9 kg 360 ml) coconut oil

28 oz. (.5 kg 360 ml) palm or hardened vegetable oil

56 oz. (1.35 kg 240 ml) olive oil

4 oz. (120 ml) wheat germ oil

2,000 IU vitamin E oil

½ cup (.12 L) calendula flower petals

4 tbs. (60 ml) almond oil

4 tbs. (60 ml) lemon grass essential oil

TOOLS AND MATERIALS

Caution: Do not use soap-making utensils for food preparation.

Cardboard box, approximately 24½ x 13½ x 5" (62 x 34 x 12.5 cm)

Wax paper

Masking tape

Rubber gloves and safety goggles or glasses

Measuring cup

½-gallon (1.9-L) glass canning jar

1 pint (480 ml) glass canning jar

Rubber spatula

Small food-grade scale

Stove or hot plate

Two large enamel or stainless steel pots, approximately 8 quarts (7.6 L)

Cardboard

Old blankets

Brown paper bags

INSTRUCTIONS

1. Prepare the mold by lining the cardboard box with wax paper. Lay one piece flat on the bottom of the box. Then, using the masking tape, tape two pieces of wax paper on each side so the papers cover 3" (7.5 cm) up from the bottom on all sides.

2. Put on the gloves and goggles or glasses.

3. Measure 6 cups (1.5 L) of water into a ½-gallon (1.9-L) glass canning jar.

4. Measure 473 grams of lye (approx. 1⅓ cans) into the pint (480 ml) glass canning jar.

5. Pour the lye into the water and stir with a rubber spatula until the liquid is clear. ***Note:*** *This is the most dangerous part of the soap-making process and requires immediate clean-up. Always pour the lye into the water. Never use a metal spatula to stir. Since the initial chemical reaction of lye to water will make this mixture very hot, approximately 200°F (90°C), set the glass jar on an appropriate surface before mixing. The mixture will cool down as it sits.* Once the mixture is clear, cover and set aside.

6. Measure the coconut oil and palm or vegetable oil into an 8 quart (7.6 L) enamel or stainless steel pot. Put it on a low heat to melt.

7. Into another 8 quart (7.6 L) enamel or stainless steel pot, measure the olive oil, wheat germ and vitamin E. (You may want to buy the vitamin E in capsule form and squeeze it out.)

8. Take the completely melted coconut oil and palm oil off the heat, then pour them into the olive oil mixture.

9. Wait until both the oil and lye mixtures are between 80-100°F (26-38°C). (The outside of the containers will be warm to the touch— or measure the temperatures with a candy thermometer.)

10. Slowly pour the lye mixture into the oil mixture. Stir constantly in a linear motion (do not stir in circles or whip).

11. Continue to stir until the mixture thickens—this will take approximately 10-15 minutes. The mixture will be ready when you can leave an upraised trail from tracing the spatula on the surface of the mixture.

12. Measure and add the almond oil, lemon grass oil, and calendula flowers one at a time, stirring between each addition. Then stir until fully blended.

13. Pour the mixture into the wax paper-lined cardboard mold. Do not scrape the sides of the pot. Cover the mold with additional cardboard, and place blankets on top to keep the soap warm so it will cool slowly. Set aside for three to five days. Note: Since it will take the soap approximately 24 hours to harden, it's best to place the mold in an area where it will be undisturbed for the first day. Otherwise, it will be difficult to move the mold while the soap is still soft.

14. After three to five days, uncover the soap and let it harden another three to five days.

15. Remove the top white layer of soap by pulling a metal ruler or scraper over the top. You should remove approximately ⅛" (.3 cm) which is the layer of caustic ash or lye residue. The soap underneath should be a smooth yellowish-orange color.

16. Divide the large block of soap into the desired size of individual bars. Measure with a ruler, then score the lines with a knife before cutting. With a sharp knife, and using a ruler as a guide, cut straight down into the soap.

17. Either lift out each individual bar by pulling up on the wax paper, or gently flip the entire box upside down to release the soap from the mold. Peel off the wax paper.

18. Place the bars right side up on the unprinted side of brown paper bags. Leave enough space between bars so they do not touch. Let the bars sit like this for three weeks. You can place the brown bags on cardboard or in boxes so you can move the bars of soap as needed while they cure.

19. Wrap each bar in muslin or pretty cotton cloth and raffia ribbon.

Designer: Beth Herdman

Personalized Gift Boxes

You've made the gift, now what about the box? Have just as much fun creating personalized gift boxes as you had in making the gift. You may even want to make a few extra boxes to use at home for organizing items on a desk or dresser top.

Designer: Traci Dee Neil-Taylor

53

MATERIALS

Papier-mâché or simple wood boxes of various shapes and sizes

Any objects to glue to the surface or cover of box

Glue, a strong adhesive works best

INSTRUCTIONS

1. Purchase inexpensive, plain boxes from a craft store. The boxes can be made of paper, wood, or papier-mâché.

2. Find items that the recipient might like, such as buttons for the sewing lover, coffee beans for the coffee lover, naturals for the gardener, etc.

3. If desired, paint the box.

4. Glue the objects to the top of the box, or decorate the box all around.

5. Be as creative as you want. Experiment with mixing objects. Incorporate small bits of fabric such as netting, lace, and ribbon. Make a small photo collage on the cover, or all the way around. Think of the box as your blank canvas and decorate at will.

Ideas for Additional Items:

Dried flowers

Cinnamon sticks

Mosaic tiles

Beans

Marbles

Beads

Charms

Old jewelry pieces

Bow and Tie

This decorated hair bow and tie make a glittery gift for a girl. Designer Ellen Zahorec says all you need is a steady hand and the patience to make hundreds of dots

54

Designer: Ellen Zahorec

MATERIALS

Black fabric hair bow

Black clip-on tie (found in the boys' department)

Glitter dimensional fabric paint

TOOLS

Pencil

Tailor's carbon paper and wheel

INSTRUCTIONS:

1. Create a design, then copy it onto the bow and tie using light pencil marks or tailor's carbon paper and wheel.

2. With the lines as a guide, use the glitter dimensional paints to complete your design.

Fabric-Covered Photo Album

A photo album is more than a place to store old snapshots—it's a treasure chest filled with family memories. Create a beautiful setting for your photographs with this elegant album. You can customize the fabric for special presentations such as a baby, wedding, or anniversary theme.

55

MATERIALS

1 loose-leaf, metal-ring photo album 11 x 12 x 2" (28 x 30.5 x 5 cm)

½" (1.5 cm) quilt batting, 26 x 14" (66 x 35.5 cm)

Fabric to cover the album as follows:

    1 piece 26 x 14" (66 x 35.5 cm)

    1 piece 14½ x 12" (37 x 30.5 cm)

    1 piece 9½ x 12" (24 x 30. 5 cm)

70" (1.7 m) decorative flat braid trim

36" (.9 m) long cord with tassels (this was purchased as a ready-made curtain tie-back)

TOOLS

Scissors

Hot glue gun

Iron

INSTRUCTIONS

1. Lay the album open on top of the quilt batting so that a ½" (1.5 cm) edge of the batting shows around the outer edges of the album.

2. With the hot glue gun, glue the batting to the inside of the album along all the edges, clipping around the metal ring holder where necessary.

3. Take the 26 x 14" (66 x 35.5 cm) piece of fabric and lay it wrong-side up. Position the open, batting-covered album on it, leaving a ½ to ¾" (1.5 to 2 cm) edge around the album.

4. Glue the fabric edges over the batting edges and to the inside edge of the album, again clipping around the metal ring holder where necessary.

5. Glue the decorative braid to the album across the four outer corners and along the front and back, ¾" (2 cm) from the spine. The ends of the cord will extend into the inside by approximately 2" (5 cm).

6. Take the two pieces of remaining fabric and iron under ½" (1.5 cm) around all the edges.

7. Lay the pieces over the inside covers of the album with the ironed edges facing down. Center the pieces, making sure they cover all raw edges. Glue to the album.

8. Tie the tassel cord around the spine of the book so the tassels dangle at either the top or bottom, outer edge of the spine.

Tip: The size of the fabric and batting will vary with the size of the photo album you use and its construction. If you're not sure of the sizes you'll need, make a paper pattern first before cutting the fabric.

Designer: Lisa Sanders

56 *Organize a Memory*

*M*ost people who lose their homes to fire or natural disasters lament that they didn't have time to save their photographs. More than mere pictures, snapshots chronicle the love we share with others throughout our lives.

Often these treasures end up in large envelopes, shoe boxes, and plastic bags that are stored under a bed, in the corner of a closet, or up on a shelf. They're victims of the modern-day time crunch, last on a long list of to-get-to-someday-when-you-have-the-time projects.

Present a certificate for a gift of time to organize someone's photographs, and it's as if you're handing them a buried treasure. Purchase or make a photo album (see page 68) and get to work. If you're doing this for an older relative, you just might learn interesting anecdotes about your family history as you sort through the photos to identify faces and places.

anise hops (*Agastache foeniculum*)

bee balm (*Monarda didyma*)

borage (*Borago officinalis*)

calendula, pot marigold (*Calendula officianlis*)

chamomile (*Matricaria recutita*)

chives, common chives (*Allium schoenoprasum*)

chrysanthemum (*Chrysanthemum* spp.)

dianthus, pinks, carnation (*Dianthus* spp.)

dill, dill weed (*Anethum graveolens*)

elderberry (*Sambucus* spp.)

English daisy (*Bellis perennis*)

fennel (*Foeniculum vulgare*)

hollyhock (*Alcea rosea*)

hyssop (*Hyssopus officinalis*)

lilac (*Syringa* spp.)

nasturtium (*Tropaeolum* spp.)

pansies (*Viola wittrockiana*)

rocket, arugula, rucola (*Eruca vesicaria*)

rose petals (*Rosa* spp.)

rosemary (*Rosmarinus officinalis*)

runner bean, scarlet runner bean (*Phaseolus coccineus*)

scented geranium (*Pelagornium* spp.)

squash blossoms (*Cucurbita* spp.)

tangerine gem, lemon gem marigolds (*Targetes tenuifolia*)

violets (*Viola* spp.)

Edible Flowers

Giving a gift of flowers is a universal way to tell someone you love them. For a slightly different bouquet, try incorporating edible flowers into a festive meal. You can use them in salads (as shown on page 71) as colorful garnishes, or as a unique decoration for a memorable cake. In preparing the flowers, treat them as you would salad greens, gently washing and drying them before use. The following list contains the common and scientific names of flowers that are safe to eat.

57

Cake Design: Jane Tomlinson
Flowers: Vicki Baker

INGREDIENTS

White vinegar

Fresh herbs

White wine vinegar

In addition you will need:

1-gal. (4.5-L) glass jar with top

12-oz. (340 g) glass bottles with tops or corks

Paraffin wax—optional

INSTRUCTIONS

1. Pour the white vinegar into a large, clean, glass jar, a 1-gallon (4.5-L) jar works best. Place clean, dry, fresh herbs in the vinegar. Seal the jar, place the jar in the sun, and let steep for 24 hours.

2. Strain the vinegar, removing the steeping herbs.

3. Sterilize the smaller bottles before use. Into the cooled, sterilized bottles place fresh, clean herbs.(After you wash the herbs, dry them with a paper towel to remove all water.) The combination of herbs and spices that you place in the jar can be different from those used for steeping.

4. Add 3 tablespoons of white wine vinegar to each bottle, then fill the bottles the rest of the way with the strained, herb-infused white vinegar.

5. Seal the bottles with a cork or bottle top.

6. You may want to add a decorative touch to the bottles by sealing the top with paraffin wax. To do this, use a double boiler to melt the wax. If you want colored wax, add bits of crayons to the paraffin. Turn the closed bottles upside down and dip the tops into the melted paraffin several times.

Herbalist Vicki Baker has created the two vinegars shown here:

4 Basil contains lemon, sweet cinnamon, and purple basil. It's good on any tomato dish, with beef or liver, on pasta, or as salad dressing

Thai Pepper begins with vinegar steeped with purple basil, then is bottled with Thai peppers, dill, rosemary, basil blooms, and summer savory. Use as a salad dressing, in dip, or in chili.

Herbal Vinegars

58

Use herbs grown in your own garden to create all-natural vinegars for use as marinades, vegetable and salad dressings, or as zesty complements to dips and sauces.

Designer: Vicki Baker

Handmade I Love You Cards

A collection of handmade cards makes a thoughtful gift that can be given throughout the year for any occasion. Your loved one will especially appreciate the time you took to gather together the little treasures that you've collected on a special walk or vacation.

MATERIALS

Handmade paper, or decorative papers

Card stock or blank greeting cards

Envelopes

Objects found on a hike or vacation with your "best friend" (ex.: feathers, leaves, flowers, little shells)

Colored pencils, crayons or paints

Rubber cement

INSTRUCTIONS

1. Making paper can be an excellent project to enjoy with a good friend or loved one. The directions provided on page 73 are for a relatively easy method. If you don't care to make your own paper, many interesting varieties are available in craft or art stores. You will also find that you can be creative with colored tissue paper, torn watercolor papers, newspapers, or whatever paper you choose.

2. Gather your materials, and, on a large work surface, begin to play by arranging found objects and torn paper shapes into pleasing arrangements.

3. When something "clicks" for you, attach items carefully with rubber cement. Experiment by adding more color with pencils, crayons or paints. Remember, sometimes less is a lot more!

4. Sign the front of the artwork if you like and definitely write a note on the back of the card with a title or date.

Designer: Susan Kinney

10-Step Papermaking

MATERIALS

Canvas stretchers

Non-rust screening

Bucket to soak pulp

Fibers, such as dryer lint, newspapers, etc.

Large pan—a clean cat litter pan works well

Old towels or blankets

Sheets of blue foam insulation or a waterproof surface you can use exclusively while the paper is drying

TOOLS

Wire cutters

Stapler

Hammer

Tacks

Blender

Large spoon

Small squeegee—optional

INSTRUCTIONS

1. First, you'll need to make your mold and traps. To make the mold, use canvas stretchers or inexpensive frames with openings the size of the size of the sheets of paper you want to make. Staple or tack non-rusting screen to one side of frame.

2. To make the traps, cut two or more additional sheets of screen to the same size as the opening of the frame—these will "trap" the pulp between them. If you don't have additional screen for the traps, you can use plastic needlepoint mesh that is cut to the size of the frame's opening.

3. Soak the dryer lint and newspapers in water. Other fibrous items, such as cat hair, plant stems, onion skins, and junk mail with non-shiny surfaces, can be used as well.

4. Tear (never cut) the wet lumps of lint and strips of newspaper into 1" (2.5 cm) strips. Place a small amount of the fiber in a blender with lots of water and blend briefly (30-45 seconds). If the blender begins to make a laboring noise ("groan"), remove some of the fiber and add more water. Pour the mixture into the large pan.

5. Keep blending small amounts of fiber and water, then pouring into the pan, until you have approximately a 3" (7.5 cm) depth of pulp in the pan.

6. Working over the pan, use a large spoon or your hands to scoop out the watery pulp onto the mold that is lined with one sheet of screen. The thickness of your sheet of paper is determined by the ratio of pulp to water.

7. Place a second screen on top of the pulp and press out any excess water with your hands or small squeegee.

8. Unto a folded towel or blanket, knock out the two screens which have trapped your pulp and place another towel or blanket on top. You may want to place the towel or blanket on the floor before knocking out the pulp, that way you can do "the papermaking dance." Tiptoe, jump, or jog on top of the traps until most of water is out.

9. Remove the top towel or blanket. Carefully peel off the top screen. Place the remaining screen and pulp, pulp side down on your drying surface. Working from one corner, pull off the remaining screen. If you use large sheets of blue foam insulation as a drying surface, the foam helps in this step by "grabbing" the pulp. You can also move the sheets of foam into an out-of-the-way area while the paper dries.

10. Allow the sheets to dry. If you move sheets off of the drying surface and they wrinkle, you can iron them at a low heat setting or press them between heavy books.

Pressed-Flower Pictures and Cards

63

Combining old-fashioned pressed flowers with a color copier lets you create an everlasting floral design. You can make a picture to frame, then copy it for the lovely and unique cards. Use them for special greetings when writing to those you love, or create packets of cards to give as thoughtful gifts.

Instructions for Pressed-Flower T-Shirt are on page 79

Designer: Cheri Hoefelmeyer

MATERIALS

Pressed leaves and flowers

Heavyweight paper

White craft glue

Blank cards (or use handmade paper to make your own)

Double-sided tape

TOOLS

Toothpicks

INSTRUCTIONS

1. Press the flowers following the instructions on page 79. When they're ready, lay them on the heavyweight paper and arrange them into a design.

2. Gently lift the edges of each flower or leaf with a toothpick and apply just enough glue near the stem or fatter portion of the leaf to "tack" in place. You do not want to apply the glue where it will seep through and show. Let dry.

3. At this stage you can mat or frame your design. For a longer-lasting colorful image that is less fragile, go to a copy shop that has a color copier, and make a copy or copies of your original work.

4. To make a card from the color copy, trim the print to a size that will fit on the blank card. Next, put a tiny piece of doubled-sided tape on each corner of the back of the print and press the print onto a card. You can glue the print to the card, just make sure you do not use too much glue and that you apply it evenly to the back of the print. For best results, use double-sided tape.

Pressed-Flower T-Shirt

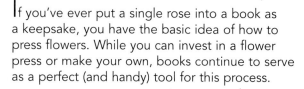

This ever-blooming design will brighten someone's life throughout the year. Not only will they appreciate the lovely floral design, whenever they wear it they'll think of you

Photo on page 78

MATERIALS

Heavyweight paper

Pressed flowers and leaves

White glue

One, 100% cotton, white, or light-colored T-shirt

TOOLS

Toothpicks

INSTRUCTIONS

1. Lightly sketch or trace an outline of a heart onto heavy paper.

2. Arrange the pressed flowers and leaves as you desire on top of the outline.

3. Using a toothpick, lift the edges of the flowers and tack them in place. For best results, place a tiny dot of glue under the stem or thicker part of the flower.

4. Make a color copy of your design on heat-transfer paper You can also have smaller color copies made of your design to use for note cards (see page 78).

5. Transfer the copy onto your shirt. For best results use a high-heat transfer press. Many copy shops have their own, or you can take your copy and shirt to a T-shirt shop where they will use their press to make the transfer.

6. Turn the finished shirt inside out whenever you wash or iron it.

Pressed Flowers

If you've ever put a single rose into a book as a keepsake, you have the basic idea of how to press flowers. While you can invest in a flower press or make your own, books continue to serve as a perfect (and handy) tool for this process.

Time gives most pressed blooms a delicate and faded beauty of their own. If you want to preserve the vibrant colors of the flowers for memory's sake or to make cards or a T-shirt, glue freshly dried flowers to heavyweight paper and copy the design using a color copier (see page 78).

Experiment pressing different flowers and leaves to see which ones will hold their color and shape more than the others. You're sure to find your own favorites.

To begin, gather fresh flowers and leaves after the dew has evaporated. The flowers and leaves must be dry when you press them to avoid mold. Next, lay individual flowers or leaves as flat as possible on a double thickness of newspaper that you've laid in between the pages of a large, heavy, hard-cover book. Sometimes laying the flowers face down works best.

Place as many flowers on the paper as will fit within the book's pages. If the book is thick enough, 2-3 inches (5-7.5 cm), you can insert another layer or two of flowers to press. Close the book, stacking several heavy books on it.

After one week, check to see if the flowers are dry; they should feel like paper. If dry, keep the flowers in the newspaper and slip them from the pages of the book. Store the flowers flat in layers in a dark, dry area such as an attic. Never store pressed flowers in a plastic bag—the plastic may cause condensation that will dampen the dried flowers and make them moldy.

Designer: Cheri Hoefelmeyer

Market Basket

A little spray paint and a dynamic design can transform a simple market basket into a decorative treasure. Fill the basket with flowers from your garden and present it to a friend who's in need of loving cheer.

65

Designer: Ellen Zahorec

MATERIALS

Market basket—look at your local farmer's market for these plain fruit baskets

Spray paint in colors of your choice

Enamel pens

Dimensional paint

INSTRUCTIONS

1. If the basket is dirty, wash it and let it dry thoroughly away from any heat source.

2. When dry, spray the basket with spray paint in a color of your choice.

3. With the enamel pens, draw the design on the basket following the design shown in the photo—or create your own. You may want to practice drawing your design on a piece of paper. Then, use a pencil to lightly draw guidelines on the basket that you can trace over with the enamel pens.

4. Use the dimensional paint to make the raised dots.

MATERIALS

Assorted handmade papers

Craft glue

Small beads

Clear acrylic medium,
in either spray can or bottle

Earring backs and pin backs

TOOLS

Scissors

Beading needle

Beading thread

Small paintbrush

Paper Jewelry

66

Use the wonderful handmade papers available today at art- and craft-supply shops to make sets of matching earrings and pins. The sewn bead details add extra texture and color interest to the surface design.

Designer: Nancy McGaha

INSTRUCTIONS

1. Select a piece of paper to be used as the base. Cut or tear it into a pleasing shape.

2. From other papers of contrasting color, cut or tear pieces smaller than the base. Arrange the smaller pieces on the base in a pleasing design, then glue them onto the base.

3. Arrange a few beads into a pleasing design. Thread the needle and string the beads. Sew the beads onto the paper in a design of your choice.

4. When the design is complete to your satisfaction, use the acrylic medium to seal, protect, and add body to the paper. Using either a spray formula or liquid from a bottle, spray or paint the front and back of each piece, applying two to three coats on each side. Do one side first, allowing the medium to dry thoroughly before turning to coat the other side.

5. Glue earring backs to the earrings or a pin back onto the pin.

MATERIALS

Velvet cut into a circle with a 16" (40 cm) diameter

Lining cut into a circle with a 16" (40 cm) diameter

Lining cut into two circles, each with a 12" (30 cm) diameter

¼" (.5 cm) wide x 53" (1.3 m) long gold braid

38" (95 cm) long gold cord

2 tassels

Glue

TOOLS

Scissors

Needle and thread

Tailor's chalk or markers

Sewing machine

INSTRUCTIONS

1. Place the 16" (40 cm) velvet circle on the 16" (40 cm) lining circle with right sides together. With a needle and thread, use small stitches to baste them together approximately ¼" (.5 cm) from the outer edge. Leave an opening for turning.

2. Turn right sides out, then close the opening by slip stitching. Press the edges. With the sewing machine, topstitch ¼" (.5 cm) from the edge. Hand sew the gold trim to the edge of the velvet side of the circle.

3. As in Step 1, baste the two 12" (30 cm) diameter circles with right sides together, leaving an opening for turning.

4. Turn and press. Topstitch ¼" (.5 cm) from the outer edge.

5. Lay the double-layered circle of lining made in Steps 3 and 4 on the circle from Step 2, lining sides together, velvet side out. Center the smaller circle on the larger one. Baste or pin together.

Velvet Jewelry Pouch

67

This elegant velvet jewelry pouch is a perfect gift for a mother, sister, or special friend. (Don't forget yourself!) Though designed to be seen, it makes a great traveling companion. Separate sewn-in sections inside the pouch keep chains from tangling and earrings from getting lost

6. Divide the smaller circle into six equal pie-shaped sections, marking the dividing lines with tailor's chalk or a sewer's marking pen. Only mark to the outer edges of the smaller circle since the seam lines will end there.

7. On the sewing machine, change your bobbin thread to the color of the velvet, and the top thread to the color of the lining. With the lining sides up, stitch through all layers on the dividing lines you marked in Step 6. Remember, you'll only be stitching to the outer edges of the smaller circle, not to the edge of the larger circle. Back tack at the outer edges of the seams.

8. With the chalk or marker, draw a small circle with a radius of 1½" (4 cm) from the center (where all the seamlines meet) of the smaller lining circle. On the sewing machine, as in Step 7 and with lining sides up, sew around the circumference of this circle (see illustration).

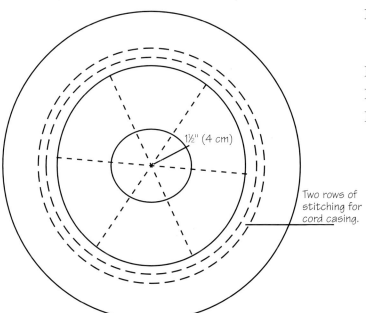

1½" (4 cm)

Two rows of stitching for cord casing.

10. Turn the circle velvet side up and cut a slit for the cord to pass through between the two lines of stitching made in Step 9.

11. Hand finish these slit edges with a buttonhole stitch.

12. Thread the cord through the casing.

13. Sew or glue the ends of the cord to the tassels (depending on the type of tassels you use). To close the pouch, draw the cord tight and tie in a bow.

Designer: Lisa Sanders

9. To make the casing for the cord, stitch a row ¼" (.5 cm) from the edge of the smaller lining circle. Stitch another row, ½" (1.5 cm) toward the outside edge from this first row of stitching (see Figure A).

Cross-Stitch Man's Mug

This coffee mug will remind someone of your love for them throughout the day. The design uses a "boy's toys" motif that gets at the heart of what he'd rather be doing with his time.

68

SIZE

10 x 3½" (25.5 x 9 cm)

140 sts wide x 49 sts high

MATERIALS

Plastic needlepoint/cross-stitch insert mug*

Vinyl cross-stitch fabric

8 colors of DMC, Kreinik, Madeira, and Anchor embroidery floss

*Used here: E-Z Stitch Coffee Mug (includes vinyl cross-stitch fabric)

TOOLS

Scissors

#22 tapestry needle

Needle threader—optional

Designer: Catherine Reurs

INSTRUCTIONS

Follow the chart and color key on page 132.

1. Locate the center of the vinyl cross-stitch fabric and the center of the design (refer to arrows on chart).

2. Separate the plies of floss, using 3 plies of DMC floss, 2 plies of Anchor Marlitt, one strand of Kreinik ¹⁄₁₆th ribbon, and one strand of Madeira Glamour in your needle.

3. Following the chart and color key, cross-stitch the design, going over one fiber intersection per stitch.

4. When all stitching is complete, place the cross-stitch fabric between the outer and inner plastic mug pieces and snap them together. To extend the life of the mug, hand wash only.

MATERIALS

24" (61 cm) lengths of fresh honeysuckle vine

Dried greens and small flowers

Raffia or ribbon

TOOLS

Scissors

Hot glue gun and glue sticks

Pin backs

Large jump rings or hanging loops

Honeysuckle Vine Pins or Ornaments

These small wreaths can be made into pins to wear any time of the year or for ornaments to adorn a holiday tree. When wrapping a gift, tie one onto your ribbon or raffia for an added surprise.

69

Designer: Cheri Hoefelmeyer

INSTRUCTIONS

1. For the pins, gather two or three 24" (61 cm) vines; for the larger ornaments, gather three to five 24" (61 cm) vines. Strip the leaves off.

2. Lay one vine length on a flat surface. Take one end of the vine and loop it down and around, forming a circle. Arrange the vine so the circle is the size you want (small for the pin, larger for the ornament) and is in the middle of the vine with two equal ends of vine extending from either side of the circle's top.

3. Starting with one end of the vine, wind it around one side of the circle, taking it in and out of the circle as you work. Tuck the end inside itself. Do the same on the other side of the circle using the other end of the vine.

4. Take another vine length and wind it completely around the circle as you did with the ends in Step 3. If you want your wreath to look fuller, wind a third vine length around the circle. For the larger ornament, you may need to wind a third, fourth, and fifth vine length around to get the fullness you desire. When the wreath is as full as you want, leave it to dry for a few days.

5. Decorate the dried vine with tiny dried flowers and leaves. Add ribbons or raffia if desired. Using a hot glue gun, glue a pin back on the back of the smaller wreath for a pin. For a larger wreath or ornament, make a long loop of raffia or attach a large jump ring for hanging.

MATERIALS

Tall glass or ceramic bottle,
an old wine bottle works best

Decorative papers

White craft glue

Paper cut into 3 x 4"
(7. 5 x 10 cm) pieces

Several pens

TOOLS

Scissors

Small brush

INSTRUCTIONS

1. Using the white glue and small brush,
   apply (collage) the papers to the bottle.

2. Place the bottle in a visible place at the
   celebration with a sign explaining its purpose.

3. Instruct the couple to wait one year before
   breaking open the bottle.

Anniversary Bottle

72

For a wedding or anniversary party,
decorate a bottle and place it on a
table. Provide small pieces of paper and
pens, then invite your friends and family to write down special thoughts about the
couple, wishes for the future, or favorite sayings
that come to mind. Have them place the papers in
the bottle, then seal the bottle with a top or cork.
Instruct the couple to save the bottle for one year,
when, on their anniversary, they may break the
bottle open to read the messages of love.

Designer: Laura Sims

73 *Grant a Wish*

*Perhaps one of the most extravagant gifts you can
give someone is to grant their wish. This gift will
always be the right size and color and is sure to
please the recipients, since they're the ones selecting
the gift.*

*Present a wish-list certificate with space for writing
five wishes. Let the recipient know you will grant one
of the wishes, though they won't know which one
until it is given, keeping an element of surprise.*

*Whether it's a request for an item, a chore, or a
favor, the recipient gets what they really want, while
you'll enjoy playing fairy godmother to those you love.*

For someone facing the daily routine in an office cubicle, vacations are a distant memory. Give them something to remember (or look forward to) by making scenic posters enlarged from vacation snapshots. Framing the poster with a simple pre-assembled frame will give the picture credibility for hanging on office walls. You can also make a photo collage from your collection of vacation pictures. Arrange the photos on a large poster board, glue them down, then frame it. If you've collected postcards, find pre-cut mats that allow you to display several pictures in one frame. Group the cards by region or country. For a more personal touch, include ticket stubs, programs, matchbooks covers, receipts, or other mementos from the trip.

For someone looking forward to a trip, give them a disposable camera as a going-away present and ask them to take scenic pictures of their trip. As part of your gift, promise them that you will create a photo poster or collage from the snapshots when they return.

Memory Stones

This simple project allows you to use a flat stone as your canvas for creating everlasting memories. Use acrylic paints to make a picture that holds special meaning for someone you love. You could choose that person's favorite animal, capture a sunset you shared together, or paint a lovely scene from your special spot. Smaller stones can be used as paperweights. Use larger stones to create interesting garden decorations. If the stone is to be used outside, you may want to coat the finished painting with several layers of clear acrylic medium.

74

Designer: Christi Hensley

Paper Heart Quilt

Have you been looking for a project that uses some of the lovely handmade papers you've seen in the art- and craft-supply stores? Designer Pei-Ling Becker shows you how with this decorative square inspired from traditional patchwork quilts.

76

Designer: Pei-Ling Becker

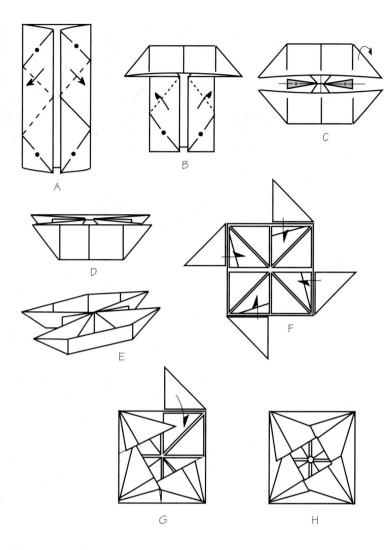

MATERIALS

Rice or handmade decorative papers

Mat board, one each, 9 x 9" (23 x 23 cm), and 16 x 16" (51 x 51 cm)

Foam core, available at craft-supply stores

Glue

TOOLS

Scissors

INSTRUCTIONS

1. Cut or tear a 10" (25 cm) square of solid-color rice or handmade paper for the background. Center and glue onto the 16 x 16" (51 x 51 cm) mat board.

2. Cut four 3" (15 cm) squares of mat board.

3. Fold five 6" (15 cm) squares of decorative paper following the steps for the "windmill" fold in the illustration. When folded, each square will measure 3 x 3" (7.5 x 7.5 cm).

4. Arrange the mat board and folded squares from Steps 2 and 3 into three rows and three columns to form a larger square following the design as shown in the photograph. Note that the mat-board squares are the bases for the hearts. When you've positioned the pieces where you want them, glue the squares to the background paper.

5. Fold or cut four heart shapes to fit on the small mat-board squares. (See the illustration on page 29 for folding instructions.)

6. To raise the hearts, cut four 1" (2.5 cm) squares of foam core. Glue the foam core pieces to the mat-board squares, then glue the hearts to the foam core.

7. Frame as you please.

Tip: You may want to practice the windmill fold on
6" (15 cm) squares of scrap paper before using
your decorative paper.

MATERIALS

Decorative paper, size 17 x 21"
(43 x 53.5 cm)

White craft glue

Wax paper

Ribbon

TOOLS

Scissors

Ruler

Pencil

Small brush

Hole punch

INSTRUCTIONS

1. With a pencil, using the ruler to measure, mark a
   point every 5" (12.5 cm) along the length of the
   paper from top to bottom. Connect the marks
   with a light line.

2. Using a "mountain fold" (convex fold), crease
   each line to make make four, 5" (12.5 cm)
   segments with a 1" (2.5 cm) surplus.

3. Applying the glue with a small brush, glue the
   1" surplus to the inside edge of side A, to form
   a rectangular box/sack with an open top and
   bottom (see Figure 1).

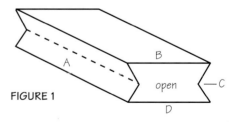

FIGURE 1

4. Using a "valley fold" (concave fold), fold sides A
   & C in half with the crease pointing toward the
   inside of the sack (see Figure 1). Flatten the sack.

5. To make the sack base, measure 2½" (6.5 cm)
   up from the bottom of the flattened sack. On
   this line, fold and crease well by folding back
   and forth one time. Open the flattened sack
   to a square form.

Wine Bag

ou've put a lot of care into
choosing the absolutely perfect
wine—now you can't seem to find a
wrapping to match the effort. When
tissue paper is too little, and a pre-purchased,
printed bag too much, make a classic handmade
bag to complete the thoughtful presentation.

77

6. Fold sides A and C in (see Figure 2). Sides B and D will fold in simultaneously to form two triangles on either end. Glue the folded triangular flaps to themselves, then glue to sides A and C to complete the base. *Note: For extra reinforcement, you may want to glue an additional square of wax paper to the inside base of the sack.*

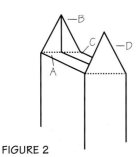

FIGURE 2

7. At the top of the sack, close the sack and punch two holes, approximatley 1½" (4 cm) apart, through both sides of the sack. Cut a length of ribbon and string it through the holes. Cut a small piece of decorative paper for a gift tag. Punch a hole in one end of the tag, then string it onto one end of the ribbon before tying a bow to close the sack.

Designer: Laura Sims

78 Create a Surprise-a-Month Club

*W*hy stop at one gift? Present a certificate for 12 related treats, each scheduled to arrive on the same day of every month. Customize the gifts to your recipient's interests or needs; think in terms of clever components. You'll find for the cost of one larger gift, you can say I love you year around.

Imagine how much a person on a special diet, such as a low-fat, no-sugar, or low-sodium plan, will appreciate a special dessert each month that meets their restrictions. Include the recipe and nutritional information so they can make their own when the last crumbs are gone.

Gardeners appreciate gifts that reflect their passion. Think of sending paper-white narcissus bulbs in January, a small gardener's hand tool in February, flower seeds in March, vegetable seeds with peat pots for starting seedlings in April, beetle traps in July, a variety of bulbs in October, and a great gardening book for December.

Making cake or candy surprises lets you experiment with new recipes each month while creating your gifts. Preserve seasonal fruits for homemade jams and jellies. Different cookies, muffins, or breads sent each month can fill several years of giving. Find interesting candles. Look for magazine subscriptions to little-known journals and special-interest magazines. Collect jokes or cartoons on related topics for the month.

If you're a poet, send poems; if you're a writer, send a new short story each month or create a continuing series sent in installments. Look for unusual teas, interesting kitchen utensils, recipes to share. Find intriguing tools or materials to help a crafter, sewer, woodworker, fly tyer, or artist. Other than money, college students love a variety of snacks; shop at value clubs and buy enough so they can share with roommates and friends. Small children will love a box of crayons with a pad of paper, watercolors, colored pencils, non-toxic, non-hardening clay, large beads to string, or coloring books.

For grandparents, parents, or friends in nursing homes, small toiletry items, colorful cards, and snapshots are always welcome. Better yet, take the time to visit once a month for the sole purpose of reading magazines, books, and favorite stories aloud. As a variation on this idea, send a box full of small individually wrapped gifts to someone recuperating from surgery or an illness. Tell them to open one gift every day until they're feeling better.

Loving Reflection Mirror

Designer Shelley Lowell created this mirror as a gift for her mother. On the back of the frame she inscribed, "You are the reflection of all the beauty in the world."

80

Designer: Shelley Lowell

MATERIALS

Plain wooden 5 x 7" (12.5 x 18 cm) frame with wide molding, either unpainted or finished

Gauze impregnated with plaster, available in craft stores

Bowl of water

Gesso

Acrylic paint—choose two to three colors that work well together

Various jewelry parts for the dangle

Head pin

Lightweight craft wire

Various beads, stones, sequins, buttons, sea shells, bells, feathers (or whatever little treasures inspire you!)

Quick-drying glue

Nail polish remover

One 5 x 7" (12.5 x 18 cm) mirror

Glazing points

Fine-point permanent marker

TOOLS

Small sponges

Small round-nose jewelry pliers

Tapestry needle

Tweezers

Cotton balls

Glazing tool

INSTRUCTIONS

1. Cut the gauze into strips that are approximately 12" (30.5 cm) long. Take one strip and dip it in the water in the bowl. Squeeze out any excess. Starting at the top of the frame, lay the gauze onto the wood, scrunching and pinching as you go. Overlap the edges slightly when starting a new strip. Leave some gauze draped over one top corner of the frame—this will give you a place to hang the dangle. Allow the gauze to dry. It could take as much as 24 hours, depending on

the weather and how wet the gauze was when you started.

2. When dry, use a clean sponge to apply the gesso to the gauze surface. Make sure it's completely covered with gesso—you may need to turn the frame upside down and around to check all the angles. Let dry.

3. Select one of the colors for a base color. Using a clean sponge, apply the base color to the gessoed surface. Again, you may need to turn the frame upside down or around to check all the angles to be sure it is completely covered with paint. Let dry.

4. Next, sponge on the second color, applying the paint lightly to some areas and heavier in others to create a blended effect. You may want to apply a third color after the second color is dry for added texture and shading.

5. Construct a dangle to hang in one of the upper corners of the gauze. This is just like making the bottom part of an earring. String various jewelry parts on a head pin, then use the round-nose pliers to make a loop at the top. You may want to take out some of your earrings for design inspiration, or you may even have a dangly earring that's lost its mate that will work.

6. To attach the dangle, take a heavy-duty needle, such as a tapestry needle, and make a hole in the gauze where you want the dangle to hang. Cut a short piece, approximately 2" (5 cm), of the lightweight craft wire. Thread the wire through the hole and into the loop of the dangle and secure. Trim wire if necessary.

7. Use quick-drying glue to attach the beads, stones and sequins. It's best to use tweezers to avoid getting the glue on your hands. I find it's helpful to have cotton balls and nail polish remover handy for cleaning glue from fingers that get stuck.

8. When you've finished decorating the frame, turn it front side down on a towel or soft surface. Lay the mirror on the back of the frame and attach it to the frame with the small glazing points, using the glazing tool.

9. With the fine-point permanent marker, write your message of love on the back of the frame.

81 Love Yourself

In the whirlwind of time spent doing for, and giving to others, it's easy to neglect a very special person—you. Loving yourself is just as important as loving others. It's said that to truly love another you must love yourself first. After all, if you don't take the time to occasionally renew and restore yourself, you won't have any mental, physical, or spiritual energy left to give to anyone else.

Susan Kinney, a potter, paper and polymer artist, and interior designer, shares ideas of gifts you can give yourself throughout the day:

- ✆ *Write a letter to yourself describing the person you would like to be—keep it handy and read it often. Start today!*

- ✆ *Drive "friendly." Aggressive driving and angry behavior only hurts you and could harm others. Besides, letting someone into your lane or line often earns you a smile from the one you've helped—instant gratification.*

- ✆ *Schedule moments of artistic or spiritual refreshment in your day. Give yourself flowers and look at them often. Take a noon stroll in the park at lunchtime. Say a prayer for a sick friend. Take yourself out on a date to a museum, movie, or special event.*

- ✆ *Celebrate life daily. Don't leave the good dishes in the cabinet, the best nightgown in the drawer, or the family jewelry or silverware locked away. Use the things that make you smile regardless of the occasion or day of the week.*

- ✆ *Forgive yourself for your yesterdays. Renew an old friendship. Write the thank-you notes you've neglected. Send a get-well card. Call or write a grieving friend, neighbor, or relative. It's easy to avoid these tasks if you've put them off—it's even harder dealing with your guilt. Don't apologize and don't procrastinate any longer, just go on from today.*

MATERIALS

3-5 varieties
of coffee

Oversized
"latte" coffee
mugs

Colored measur-
ing scoops

Beeswax

Coffee Beans

Candlewicking

TOOLS

Double boiler

Candle form

Coffee Lover's Basket

Create samplers of your favorite coffees to share with your closest coffee-loving friends. As with any gift basket, you can make this as elaborate as you want by including a variety of small coffee accessories and appliances. For true coffeehouse ambiance, make the beeswax and coffee bean candle.

82

Designer: Traci Dee Neil-Taylor

INSTRUCTIONS

1. Find an interesting basket or container to hold the ingredients.

2. Purchase different varieties of gourmet coffees for your sampler.

3. Select cups, and, if desired, colorful napkins or place mats.

4. Include biscotti or other baked treats to complement the coffee.

5. You can also add extras such as a coffee grinder, coffee press, and flavored creams.

6. To make the candle, begin by melting the beeswax in a double boiler. Fill a candle form halfway with coffee beans. Place the wick and pour the liquid beeswax into the form. Let harden, then remove the candle from the form. When lit, the candle gives off the aromatic scent of fresh roasted coffee.

MATERIALS

Variety of pasta

Homemade sauce

Dried herbs and spices

Garlic

Bread

Olive oil

Balsamic vinegar

Red checkered material

Pasta Lover's Gift Package

Ⓦhat can be any better than a meal brought to your doorstep? With this complete kit, all they'll have to do is boil the water and set the table!

83

Designer: Traci Dee Neil-Taylor

INSTRUCTIONS

1. Look for a suitably sized basket or interesting container to hold the ingredients.

2. Find interesting pasta shapes and combine them for an eclectic mix. For pasta purists, present one classic shape.

3. Make your own secret sauce, place a generous amount in a glass jar, and affix your personal label; or, buy a gourmet commercial brand.

4. Include extra dried herbs, garlic, (even dried mushrooms) so the recipient can customize the sauce to taste.

5. Add a crusty loaf of bread and separate decorative jars filled with extra virgin olive oil and balsamic vinegar (for dipping).

6. Cut the checkered fabric into simple, no-sew place mats by using a pinking shear around the edges.

7. If you're feeling particularly generous, include flowers (sunflowers, of course), imported Parmesan cheese, and a bottle of wine.

84 The Art of the Gift Basket

If you know someone's special interest or epicurean weakness, you can create a custom-made gift by assembling a basket full of items that focus on the recipient's personal pleasures. Because you're revealing how much you know about a person by the items you choose, thinking up imaginative baskets is almost as much fun as giving them away. Here are a few examples:

Tea Lover

Include a teapot for two, teacups, a tea infuser, tea cozy, a sampler of teas, and a variety of small packages or tins of cookies and biscuits that complement the beverage.

Traveler

Put together travel accessories, such as an inflatable travel pillow, combination lock, luggage tags, a money belt, city maps, and liquid detergent in a plastic bottle and large sink stopper for on-the-go laundering. If you've collected an odd assortment of foreign coins, place them in a small purse so the traveler will have instant spare change for the metro, a newspaper, or a vending machine when they reach their destination.

Sports Fan

Whether in person or at home, the sports fan wants to see the big event. If you're feeling extremely generous, make tickets the centerpiece of the basket, then include small items with the team's logo (you shouldn't have any trouble finding more than you need!) such as a T-shirt, hat, or stadium cushion. Pack the items in an insulated food bag or a small beverage cooler. For the armchair spectator, include logo items, noisemakers, pom poms, and an assortment of favorite snacks and beverages to get him through the game. Use the team colors as your guide when choosing ribbon, wrapping, or tissue paper.

Food Lovers

It's easy to assemble a basket around a food lover's particular favorite: an assortment of mustards; a selection of pastas and sauces; pancake and waffle mixes, pure maple syrup and a selection of preserves; hot salsas, chips, and chili spices; chocolate. Don't forget the dieter—include low-calorie and low-fat snacks and food substitutes along with a cookbook that features light, easy, and flavorful recipes.

Cooks

If the cook has a specialty, such as Chinese, Italian, French or Thai food, selecting related items will be easy. Combine gourmet ingredients, such as exotic spices and imported pre-packaged mixes. Add fun and interesting kitchen gadgets. Aprons, pot holders, and dish towels are also welcome items.

Basket Basics

To begin, you'll need a basket. Technically speaking, your "basket" can be any container that fits the theme: a galvanized pail, painter's paper bucket, wastebasket, stackable plastic storage cube, a tackle box, an old suitcase, a wooden vegetable crate, a watering can, and, of course, baskets of all shapes and sizes. You'll also need tissue paper, ribbon, tape, and clear or colored cellophane gift wrap. Depending on your theme, you may also use decorative gift wrap, old newspapers, or colored comic pages.

Crumple sheets of tissue paper (or old newspapers or decorative wrap) to fill the bottom of the container. This will help elevate the items as you arrange them. You may also use any pre-packaged fillers you can find at craft shops or card and stationery stores, such as spanish moss, shredded cellophane, or raffia.

Choose one large item as the focal point of the basket, arranging the smaller items around it. Use crumpled sheets of paper or filler to fill in the spaces. Attach ribbons or streamers to the container. If desired, you can wrap the basket in clear or colored cellophane, securing the top with ribbon.

Embossed Velvet Scarf

This long embossed velvet scarf makes a beautiful accessory for evening wear. Any flat object with a bold outline can be used as a pattern for embossing. Experiment with a scrap of velvet first to see how it works—and how easy it is!

85

Designer: Lisa Sanders

MATERIALS

2 yds. (1.8 m) of 36" (.9 m) wide rayon/silk blend velvet

Corded bridal lace, approximately 10" wide x 26-40" long (25.5 x 66-101.5 cm)

Thread to match color of velvet

2 tassels to match color of velvet *

* You will need tassels with a round "cap," available at stores that sell home furnishing trims and tassels.

TOOLS

Scissors

Iron and ironing board

Spray water bottle

INSTRUCTIONS

1. To get straight edges on the velvet, true the ends by pulling a thread on each end, then cutting on these lines.

2. From one end, cut a 1" (2.5 cm) strip and set aside.

3. Lay the lace on the ironing board with the corded side up.

4. Lay the velvet over the lace, velvet/nap side down. Position the velvet over the lace so there is approximately a 1" (2.5 cm) edge of velvet extending over one long edge of the lace.

5. Using the spray water bottle, moisten (do not wet) the velvet.

6. Starting at one edge, place a warm iron on the velvet, and hold it in place for approximately 20 seconds. Try not to press too hard—if you do, you'll get the impression of the iron rather than the lace. You will be able to see the impression of the lace on the wrong side of the fabric as it becomes embossed. Once you see this, use the time it took to make the impression as a guide for the length of time you need to keep the iron in place over each section.

7. Move the iron to the next position and hold it there for the determined length of time. Do not drag the iron. *Always lift the iron up and place it*

down each time you move it to the next position. If you drag the iron across the velvet, the fabric will shift and the image you're embossing will be blurred.

8. When you've completed that section, reposition the fabric over the lace so that it is 1" (2.5 cm) away from the first row of embossed velvet. Repeat Steps 5-7 on that section of velvet.

9. Emboss the other end of the velvet by repeating Steps 4-8. When completed, you should have two rows of embossed pattern at each end of the scarf.

10. Cut some of the lace motifs from the lace and position them randomly on the ironing board.

11. Lay the fabric over them, spray with water, and emboss as you did for the ends.

12. Keep repeating step 11, randomly embossing the motifs approximately 8" (20.5 cm) apart on the remaining fabric.

13. With right sides together, sew the scarf just inside and along the selvage edges. Trim the selvage seam allowance to ⅜" (1 cm), and turn the scarf right side out.

14. Sew a shirring (or basting) stitch about ½" (1.5 cm) in from each cut edge.

15. Shirr or pull the basting stitch to gather the ends.

16. With needle and thread, sew across the gathered ends to secure.

17. From the 1" (2.5 cm) wide strip of velvet cut in Step 2, cut two strips, each 1" (2.5 cm) wide and 8" (20.5 cm) long.

18. Run a shirring stitch along the long edges of each strip. Pull the stitch to gather the strips to approximately 2½" (6.5 cm) long.

19. Tuck in the raw edges by folding at the shirring, then stitch to the tassels at the base of the tassel "cap." If you are using a regular tassel without a round cap, be careful that the stitches don't show on the outside when you sew the shirred ends closed. Secure the cord end of the tassel inside the shirred ends first.

20. Sew tassels over each shirred end of scarf.

86 Give a Day

*H*ow extravagant to be able to give someone their very own day! Send Mom to the spa where she'll be pampered with a massage, manicure, pedicure, facial, and make-over. Arrange a baby-sitter for the day and have a simple take-out meal waiting when she returns.

Dads need time, too. A weekend day, free from a to-do list, will give him time to pursue a hobby, play his favorite sport, or just lounge around the house. Pack up the children and give him time to himself to enjoy peace and quiet in his own home.

Older adults will appreciate your company. Take them shopping, out to lunch, then complete the day with a late-afternoon movie. Teenagers might like time to sleep and a day without chores. Let younger children plan a day by letting them choose activities you both can share. Some ideas might be a trip to the zoo, video arcade, museum, or amusement park, time to play catch, soccer, or to fly a kite. Include a special meal at a restaurant of their choice.

Night and Day Clock

Tell someone you love them anytime of the day or night. The sun will never set on your love, and the moon is always bright for romance with this whimsical design.

87

Designer: Shelley Lowell

MATERIALS

Clock kit, available at craft stores

Round wood base made especially for clock kit

Wood filler or joint compound

Fine-grit sandpaper

Gesso

Tracing paper

Acrylic paints

TOOLS

Pencil

Brushes

INSTRUCTIONS

1. If necessary, fill in any cracks or nicks in the wood base with wood filler or joint compound. When dry, lightly sand the wood base with fine sandpaper.

2. Coat the wood base with gesso and allow to dry.

3. Draw your design directly onto the gessoed wood base. Or, if you prefer, create a design and copy it onto tracing paper. Turn the tracing paper over and trace over the lines of the design. Lay the paper on the gessoed wood, and, once more, trace over the lines to transfer the design to the surface.

4. Using the acrylic paints, paint the design onto the base.

5. Attach the clock mechanism following the manufacturer's instructions. Install the battery and set the clock.

INGREDIENTS

Pretzel rods (any shaped pretzel, fruit, or crackers will work)

Semisweet, milk, or white chocolate chips, or carob chips

Multi-colored baking sprinkles

TOOLS

Wax paper

Butter knife

Chocolate Sprinkled Pretzels

88

This is a great project to share with children—in addition to making a special treat, they'll enjoy spending time with you in the kitchen.

INSTRUCTIONS

1. Place the chocolate in a microwave-safe bowl. Melt the chocolate in the microwave. Depending on the size of your microwave, this should take 1-2 minutes. If you don't have a microwave, melt the chocolate in the top of a double boiler.

2. Hold one end of the pretzel (or fruit or cracker) while spreading melted chocolate on the opposite end.

3. Roll the pretzel in candy sprinkles and lay it on wax paper to harden.

Designer: Cheri Hoefelmeyer

Dried Orange & Cinnamon Stick Wreath

You don't have to be a cook to enjoy receiving this wreath. While its natural look makes it a decorative complement to any kitchen, its aroma—the combination of sweet, earthy cinnamon and citrus—guarantees that it will be a gift that's moved from room to room.

89

Designer: Traci Dee Neil-Taylor

MATERIALS

Oranges

Cinnamon sticks

Twine or raffia

Orange extract

TOOLS

Oven

Baking rack or cookie sheet

Skewer

Hand drill or small craft tool with drill bit

INSTRUCTIONS

1. Preheat the oven to 350°F (175°C).

2. Cut the oranges into very thin slices and lay them on a baking rack or cookie sheet.

3. Reduce the oven heat to 300°F (150°C).

4. Cook the orange slices for 2-3 hours. Check occasionally and turn over as necessary. When dried, remove from oven and allow to cool.

5. Use a skewer or piercing tool to make a small hole in the center of each dried orange slice.

6. To make holes in the cinnamon sticks, use a small hand drill or a motorized craft tool with a small drill bit. Since cinnamon sticks are brittle, drill gently—you may need to experiment with a few sticks until you get the right pressure.

7. Thread the twine or raffia through the holes in the orange slices and cinnamon sticks. Over time the aroma will begin to fade. To refresh the scent, use a few drops of orange extract or oil, applying it sparingly to the dried slices.

Tip: Follow the basic recipe using limes and lemons—they make a colorful variation. If you have a dehydrator, use it instead of the oven, following the directions for drying citrus fruit.

Feather Lamp Shade

Tickle someone's fancy every time the light goes on (or off). Made with white feathers, this shade has a classic look straight from a 1930s movie. Try brightly colored feathers for a tropical effect or peacock feathers for a touch of the exotic.

90

Designer: Lisa Sanders

MATERIALS

White feathers
(or a color of your choice)
Lamp shade

TOOLS

Glue gun and sticks

INSTRUCTIONS

1. Sort the white feathers by length into piles of short, medium, and long.

2. Starting at the bottom edge, glue the long feathers to the shade so that the ends of the feathers extend beyond the shade by 2" (5 cm).

3. Glue the remaining feathers in rows around the circumference of the shade, working from the bottom up. As you work up, gradually decrease the length of the feathers, using the shortest ones on the top rows.

4. For the last row of feathers at the top, let the quill ends extend beyond the top edge of the shade about 1–2" (1.5 cm). Trim the quill ends until they are even with the top edge of the shade.

Tip: Since most feathers have downy areas near the quill ends, try trimming the shortest feathers until they are mostly down. Use these on the last two or three rows of the shade for a more fluffy look at the top.

Pastel Floral Box

T he delicate washed colors of this box lend it a romantic look from another era. Combined with the flowers and a touch of ribbon, the box looks as if it could contain a present for a Victorian bride.

91

Designer: Louise Riddle

MATERIALS

Covered box

Silk flowers

½" (1.5 cm) wide ribbon

Glue

White matte spray paint

Chalk in pastel shades

Clear matte spray lacquer

TOOLS

Scissors

INSTRUCTIONS

1. Cut two lengths of ribbon, one approximately 2" (5 cm) longer than length of the box top, and one approximately 2" (5 cm) wider than the width of the box top. Lay the ribbons on top of the box so they cross at the center of the top. Glue them to the top and down the sides. Turn the top over and glue the remaining ends to the inside of the top, cutting away any excess.

2. Cut two lengths of ribbon, one slightly longer than the width of the bottom of the box plus twice the bottom's depth, and one slightly longer than the length of the bottom of the box plus twice the bottom's depth. Turn the bottom of the box over with the bottom facing up. Lay the ribbons on the bottom of the box so they cross at the center of the bottom. Glue them to the bottom of the box.

3. Turn the bottom over and bring the ribbons up the sides of the box, aligning them with the ribbons on the box top. Glue the ribbons to the sides of the box, cutting any excess ribbon flush to the edges of the bottom of the box.

4. Arrange the silk flowers on the top of the box. Once you have an arrangement that pleases you, glue them in place.

5. Using the spray paint, paint the inside of the box top and bottom. For best results, and to avoid drips, apply several light coats rather than one heavy one. Allow the paint to dry between coats.

6. Keeping the top and bottom separate, paint their outsides—including the flowers and ribbons—using the white spray paint. Apply several coats of paint, covering the original colors of the flowers, box, and ribbons. Again, for best results, apply several light coats, allowing the paint to dry thoroughly between each coat.

7. Color the box, including the flowers and ribbon, with the chalk. Before you begin, you may want to do a few simple sketches until you get a color scheme you like.

8. When the box is colored to your satisfaction, you'll need to seal the chalk so it won't rub off. Spray the box with the clear matte lacquer. Apply two to three coats, allowing each coat to dry thoroughly before applying the next.

Tip: The box may look delicate, but the matte lacquer will protect it for years of enjoyment. Try using this technique on picture frames for another romantic gift.

Fragrant Pepper Wreath

The Sweet Annie (*Artemnesia annua*) used

92

in this wreath has a subtle, herbal scent. If you've hesitated making a wreath for a man, try this one. He'll appreciate the peppers if he's a chili fan, while enjoying the wreath in his den or office for its masculine fragrance.

MATERIALS

Thin-gauge floral wire

200 fresh Thai hot peppers (a small, hot red pepper)

50, 6" (15 cm) stems of Sweet Annie (*Artemnesia annua*)

1 medium grapevine wreath, (or make your own with sections of vine)

Designer: Vicki Baker

INSTRUCTIONS

1. Before arranging your wreath, string the peppers. This is much easier than stringing peppers that are already dry. Cut four 12" (30.5 cm) pieces of floral wire. String 50 peppers on each of the wires. Hang to dry.

2. Weave stems of Sweet Annie (artemnesia annua) into the grapevine wreath until the wreath is evenly decorated, but not completely covered. The exposed grapevine complements the rest of the design.

3. Take the peppers that are dried on the wire and shape them into spirals and position on the wreath. Wrap extra floral wire around the strings and though the wreath to hold them in place.

Needlepoint Dancing Cats Frame

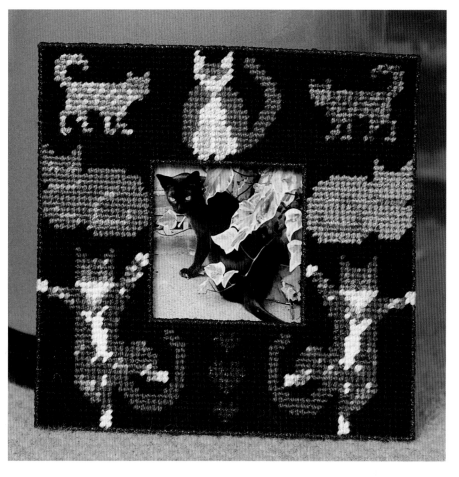

Any true cat lover likes to keep a picture of their fantastic feline close to their heart all day. Whether you love a cat lover, or love your cat, you won't be able to resist making this joyous photo frame

93

SIZE
7 x 7" (18 x 18 cm)
69 sts wide x 68 sts high

MATERIALS
One piece of 10-count mesh clear-plastic canvas

14 colors of Anchor, Kreinik, Madeira, and Paternayan yarns

TOOLS
Scissors
#18 tapestry needle
Needle threader—optional

Designer: Catherine Reurs

INSTRUCTIONS
Follow the chart on pages 134–135 which includes the yarn specifications and color key.

1. Locate the center of the plastic canvas and the center of the design (refer to arrows on chart). Counting squares to measure, cut the large square from the center of the mesh.

2. Following the chart and color key, use the continental stitch throughout, going over one "bar" per stitch.

3. Use one complete strand (all three plies) of Paternayan Persian wool; two strands Kreinik #16 braid; four strands of Madeira Glamour; and two strands of Anchor #3 Perle Cotton in your needle.

4. To keep the needlepoint frame stiff, you can either glue the needlepoint frame to a pre-made frame of similar dimensions or glue it to a piece of cardboard or mat board that is cut slightly smaller than the needlepoint frame.

Embroidered Felt Table Runner

Designer Terry Taylor made this table runner in honor of his parent's 50th wedding anniversary. He calls the design "Two Hearts As One." The use of tongue-shaped appliqué pieces and simple embroidery stitches were inspired from the traditional penny rug technique. Terry incorporates the buttonhole and Algerian stitch—which are actually easy straight stitches— however, he says you may want to try other simple stitches such as lazy daisy or French knots.

94

MATERIALS

5 colors of felt yardage *

1 yard (.9 m) of the felt will be used for the base of rug, figure more if you choose to make a row of your "tongues" in the same color.

Heavyweight cardboard for tongue pattern

Perle cotton & metallic embroidery thread

Newspaper or other paper to cut out hand pattern

Sewing or quilting thread to match backing material

* Originally, felted wool fabrics from old clothing were used to make penny rugs. This project can be made using felt yardage as well. For this piece I used a combination of recycled fabric (the green, beige, and maroon were skirts) and felt yardage. You can make your own felt from a favorite old wool suit or skirt. First remove the linings, buttons, etc. before taking the suit apart at the seams. Next, wash the pieces in the washing machine using warm soapy water. Then dry the pieces in the dryer on a moderate to hot setting.

TOOLS

Pencil

Sharp scissors

Fabric pencil or chalk

Needle suitable for thread chosen

Straight pins or quilter's pins

INSTRUCTIONS

Patterns for this design are on pages 136–137.

1. Determine the size of the finished piece you wish to create. The base of the piece shown is a 24 x 32" (61 x 81.5 cm) oval. You could make a rectangular or square shape as desired.

2. Make a pattern by sketching a large oval (or the desired shape) on a large piece of paper, then cut it out. Pin this pattern to the material you've chosen for your base, then cut the material out.

3. Transfer the "tongue" pattern found on page 137 onto heavy cardboard. Cut it out.

4. Using a fabric pen or chalk, trace the tongue pattern onto the material you've chosen for the outside edge of the piece. The number of tongues you'll need depends on the size and shape of your base. Don't spend time counting and measuring to determine how many you'll need—just cut a bunch and lay them along the outside edge of your shape without overlapping until you have enough to go around the edge.

5. Once you know how many tongues you'll need for the first row, you can estimate the number needed to complete the other two rows. Trace, then cut out the rest of the tongue shapes from the other colors of felt. Don't worry that you'll cut too many—it's better to have more to choose from than not enough.

6. For each tongue, work around the edge in perle cotton using a buttonhole stitch—don't work the flat end, leave it unadorned. Once you find the rhythm stitchers tend to develop as they work, you might find it easier to embroider all the tongues at once.

7. Work the Algerian stitch on each tongue. Center the stitches, with the bottom of the stitch beginning ½" (1.5 cm) up from the bottom edge of the tongue.

8. When you have completed embroidering all the tongues, you can begin work on the center portion of the rug. Enlarge the pattern of the two hands found on page 136 to suit the size runner you're making. Trace it onto the material you've selected for the center, then cut it out.

9. To assemble the rug, begin by placing the outer row of tongues around the edge—do not overlap. On the next two rows, you will slightly overlap the edges of the tongues. Lay the second row down, overlapping as shown in the photograph, then lay the last, innermost row, continuing to overlap as you go.

10. Lay and position the center portion. Adjust the tongues as needed to cover the backing material. The center oval should cover the flat edge of the innermost row of tongues. When you are satisfied with the placement, remove all but the outer row and carefully pin the outer row in place.

11. Use a small running stitch or buttonhole stitch to attach the outer row to the backing material. Remove the pins.

12. Place and pin the tongues on the next row and repeat Step 10. Do the same for the innermost row.

13. Pin the outer edge of the center portion to the base material, being careful to cover the flat ends of the tongues. Using a buttonhole stitch that catches the base material, attach the center portion around all edges to the runner.

14. Cut out additional heart and teardrop shapes as desired to accent the center portion (patterns on page 137). For a raised effect, cut two shapes, one slightly larger than the other. Lay the smaller shape on top of the larger one. Position them on the center portion and attach them by stitching the center with your chosen embroidery stitch through all layers of fabric. Work the buttonhole stitch around the edges of the shapes.

15. Use a long running stitch underneath the tongues to tack them in place and keep them from flapping.

Decorative Covered Boxes

Why spend time meticulously wrapping a gift with beautiful paper that will only be discarded? With a little extra time and effort, you can use decorative paper to cover a lidded box—then once the gift is given, the box assumes another life as a lovely storage container.

95

MATERIALS

Lidded box

Decorative paper

White craft glue

TOOLS

Ruler or tape measure

Pencil

Scissors

Artist's paintbrush

Designer: Laura Sims

Silk Flower Monogrammed Cushion

T his silk pillow makes a sumptuous gift that will be equally welcome in a bedroom or formal living area. The floral monogram lends the ultimate touch of personal luxury

97

MATERIALS

1 silk hydrangea bush

10 x 9" (25.5 x 23 cm) piece of embroidery canvas or buckram

17" (43 cm) square of dupioni silk

72" (1.8 m) of cord trim with edge

4 tassels to match the cord color

16 x 17" (40.5 x 43 cm) rectangle of dupioni silk

2½ x 17" (6.5 x 43 cm) rectangle of dupioni silk

16" (40.5 cm) zipper

16 x 16" (40.5 x 40.5 cm) foam or polyester-fill cushion insert

TOOLS

Paper and pencil

Black marker

Scissors

Thimble

Needle and thread

Sewing machine

INSTRUCTIONS

1. With paper and pencil, sketch an initial until you get a shape and size of letter that pleases you. The "S" initial for this pillow is 9" (23 cm) long by 6" (15 cm) wide. Keep the initial drawing simple—any fancy embellishments on the letter may not show up once you lay your flowers on the outline. Trace over the initial with black marker.

2. Lay the embroidery canvas or buckram over the initial and trace the image in pencil onto the canvas.

3. Cut the individual berries, leaves, and hydrangea flowers off of the bush. Arrange the flowers on the canvas over the letter you've traced. When you're pleased with the arrangement, sew them by hand onto the canvas along the initial's outline. Since you'll be hand stitching through the plastic base of the silk flowers, a thimble and strong needle are recommended. Take a few leaves from the bush, trim, then sew them randomly to the initial. Do the same with the berries.

4. Turn the canvas over and carefully trim around the stitching so that you are left with the initial's shape.

5. Center the floral initial on the right side of the 17" (43 cm) silk dupioni square. Pin, then hand sew the initial onto the silk, working from the wrong side of the silk, until it is secure.

6. With the right side of the silk square facing up, position the braid ½" (1.5 cm) from the edge of the silk, then baste (see illustration). Allowing for a ½" (1.5 cm) seam allowance, basting the braid in this position will place the braid on the edge of the pillow once it's sewn and turned.

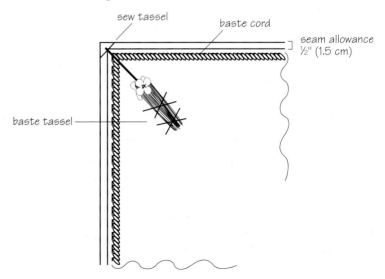

sew tassel

baste cord

seam allowance ½" (1.5 cm)

baste tassel

7. Take four hydrangea flowers and sew one onto the top band of each tassel. Sew the tassels onto each corner of the right side of the 16" (40.5 cm) square. Baste over the tassel to keep it free of the seam (see illustration).

8. Sew the 16 x 17" (40.5 x 43 cm) and the 2½ x 17" (6.5 cm x 43 cm) pieces of dupioni silk together along their 17" (43 cm) edges.

9. Using a lapped application, insert the zipper so the lapped edge will face toward the bottom of the cushion.

10. With right sides together, sew the front and back of the pillow together. Leave the zipper partially open to help when turning the corners as you sew.

11. Open the zipper completely, and turn the cushion right side out.

12. Insert 16 x 16" (40.5 x 40.5 cm) cushion and zip closed.

13. Remove the basting thread on the tassels.

Tip: Any small silk flowers of your choice should work as well as the hydrangeas.

Designer: Lisa Sanders

Hearts in flight

Express your high-flying feeling of love for someone when you make this colorful, whimsical, and easy-to-make mobile. By combining beautiful decorative papers with several coats of gloss medium for extra shine, you're sure to catch the eye and capture the heart of the one you love.

Designer: Claudia Lee

MATERIALS

Cardboard

Decorative papers in colors of your choice

Acrylic gloss medium

Dimensional paint

TOOLS

Scissors

Paintbrush, 1" (2.5 cm) wide

Piercing tool (ice pick or large needle)

Clear fishing line

INSTRUCTIONS

Patterns for this design are on page 138.

1. Copy the patterns onto the cardboard and cut out. Feel free to make up your own design or to alter the ones presented here. The basic idea is to have a large enough main shape from which to hang several smaller ones. With a mobile, it's all in the balance— you'll need to hang the same number of pieces of equivalent size on each side.

2. Using the cardboard as patterns, trace the shapes on the decorative papers and cut out. The hanging pieces need to be fairly heavy. Glue two pieces of paper together for extra body and to double the weight. Remember that both sides of the paper will show.

3. Using the paintbrush, apply two coats of gloss medium to both sides of each shape, allowing the gloss to dry thoroughly between coats.

4. Outline the shapes with dimensional paint, allowing it to dry completely before proceeding.

5. Lay your finished shapes on a table, arranging them until you have an overall design that pleases you. Remember the balance!

6. With an ice pick or large needle, pierce a hole in the edge of each piece.

7. Tie fishing line to a small shape, then tie it to a larger shape. Do the same on the other side. Work back and forth from side to side until all shapes are attached. To check the balance, hold the mobile up from the large, main shape. Untie the fishing line and readjust the balance as needed.

99 *Children*

*T*oday's children have a hard time deciding what they want. Television commercials, product tie-ins associated with popular movies, and advertisements in magazines, comic books, and on billboards provide a barrage of enticements more tempting than candy on a witch's house. While giving children the toy of their dreams will make them happy for a short time, it's the gift of yourself that they'll remember after the toy's broken or long forgotten.

In busy households it's often a luxury to have a leisurely dinner or time to watch a movie. Schedule a family night where undivided attention goes only to being together. If life is too hectic, schedule a chore day and make it a celebration of family unity—do yard work, clean the house, or go grocery shopping together. Even the smallest member of the family can have a job to do. At the end of the day, order pizza or a favorite take-out meal.

Spend time with each child once a month to give siblings equal time with Mom and Dad. Set up "dates" that involve one parent, one child. Make it a special age-appropriate time—a trip to a museum, the theater, community event, or a nature hike.

If you don't have children of your own, there are many opportunities for positively affecting the life of a child. Become a mentor, a tutor, a Big Brother or Sister, read stories to day care groups, become a children's tour guide at an art or natural history museum, or coach a sports or academic team.

Silk Flower Swag for the Office

While women are accustomed to receiving flowers, men are often overlooked when it comes to floral gifts. It's not that men dislike flowers, it's just that sometimes they look too flowery.

100

Designer: Lisa Sanders

This handsome arrangement was designed with men in mind. The muted colors and rich details make it suitable for an office setting.

MATERIALS

Floral wire

1 long garland of silk grape leaves

2 stems of small red or yellow berries

2 bunches of grapes

2 stems of blackberries

2 stems of loganberries

3 dried pomegranates

3 green wired-wood floral picks

3 branches of eucalyptus

1 bunch of red-backed green leaves

1 bunch of moss-colored oblong leaves

1 stem of a large beige rose and bud

2 stems of ranunculus in shades of beige

Cord and tassels, purchased as ready-made curtain tie-backs

36" (.9 m) cord

TOOLS

Scissors

Needle or piercing tool

INSTRUCTIONS

1. Cut the floral wire into 6–8" (15-20.5 cm) lengths. You will need many of these pieces, so cut them all at once to have them handy.

2. Form the grape-leaf garland to a length of 46" (1.1 m). Depending on the length, you may need to double the garland back on itself. Secure the garland with floral wire.

3. Using the center of the garland as a focal point, begin to lay the red berries along the grape branches toward the ends. Overlap the stems of the berries with the stems of the garland.

4. Cut two small branches of red or yellow berries and wire them close to the center of the garland.

5. Wire each bunch of grapes to the garland. Position them slightly off center with one closer to the center and one closer toward one end.

6. Wire the blackberries onto the garland, with each stem close toward opposite ends. Position them more toward the center than the red or yellow berries.

7. Wire the loganberries, one stem on each side, closer to the center than the blackberries.

8. You will now have many stems and branches running parallel with the length of the garland. Wire the stems together, then at five to seven places along the garland, wire the bunches of stems to the garland to help keep it together and make it sturdy.

9. Using a piercing tool or needle, pierce a hole in each pomegranate on its underside. Into each hole, insert a green, wired-wood floral pick so the end of the wooden stake with the wire attached is exposed.

10. Wire the pomegranates to the garland. Position one slightly off center to the right, one at the end on the right, and one about halfway down the left branch of the garland.

11. Layer in the eucalyptus branches and wire them to the garland.

12. Add other colored leaves throughout the garland as desired.

13. Place the big rose and bud at the center of the garland and secure it with wire.

14. Place each group of two ranunculus at the middle to outer ends of the garland and wire to the garland.

15. Drape the cord and tassels around the garland at each end and secure with wire. Weave another yard (.9 m) of cord in and out of the leaves so it drapes down in a few places on the garland. When you are satisfied with the position of the drape, wire the cord to the garland.

16. To make a loop for hanging, cut three pieces of floral wire into 10" (25.5 cm) sections, then twist them together to form one length. Bend this length in half to form a loop. Twist the ends together approximately 2" (5 cm) from the top of the loop, twisting until there is a tight twist approximately ¼" (.5 cm) long. Do not twist the remaining ends of the length together.

17. To prevent the garland from hanging off center, find its center of gravity before attaching the loop. To do this, hang the garland off the end of your index finger and adjust its position until it feels balanced. This point may not correspond to the visual center of the design, but it's the point where you want to attach the loop you made in Step 16.

18. Position the loop so it does not show above the leaves with the loop pointing up. Wire the loop securely onto the garland.

Tip: Use your "eye" to judge just where to add each fruit, leaf, or flower. A combination of symmetry with only a few items placed asymmetrically works best. Don't hesitate to bend the leaves and branches a bit to get a shape you like.

Transfer Patterns for Large
and Small Wood Letter Openers

roughed up
areas

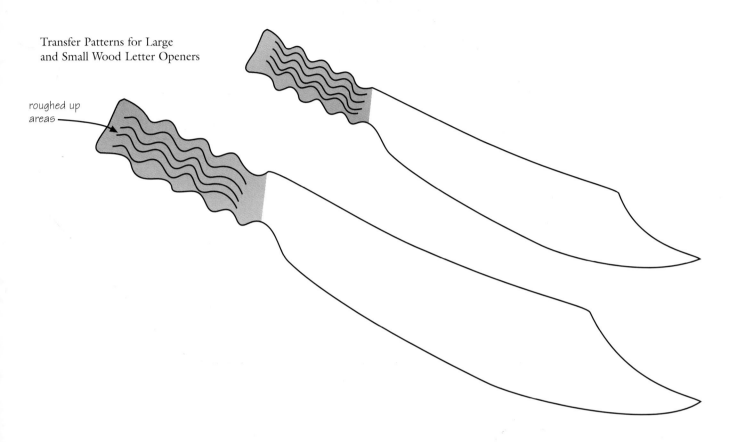

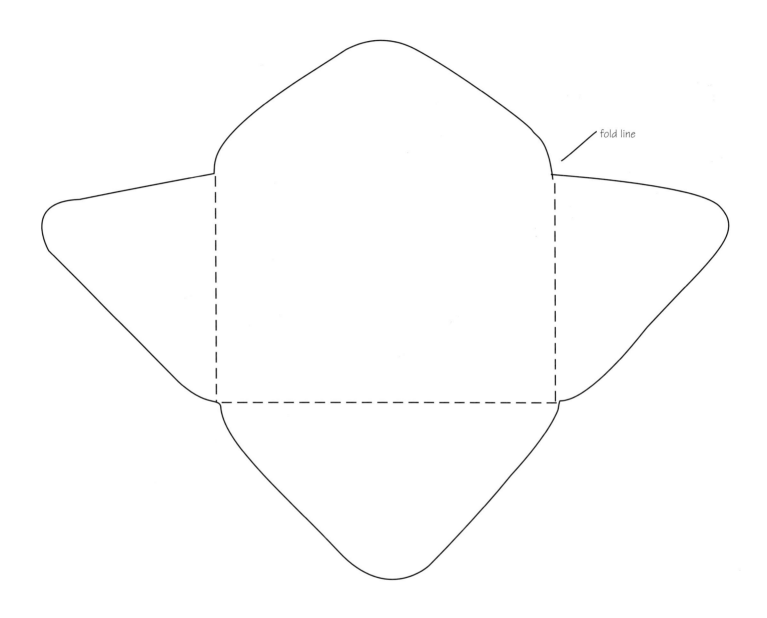

fold line

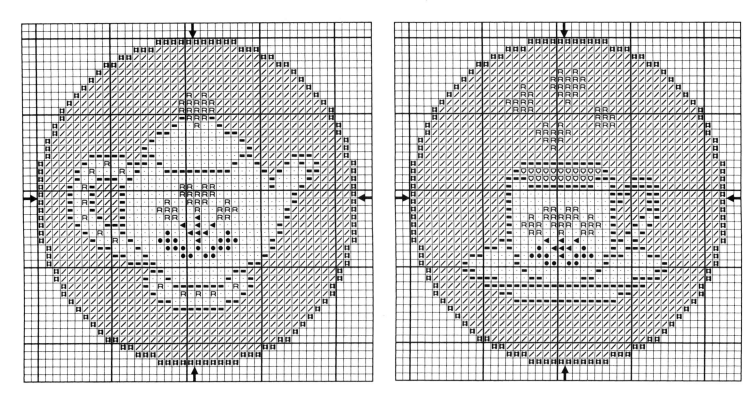

COLOR KEY

Symbol	Fiber Name	Number	Color	Amount
·	Anchor Marlitt	800	White	1 skein
/	Anchor Marlitt	836	Blue	1 skein
⊟	Madeira Glamour	2415	Dark Red	1 spool
R	Madeira Glamour	2414	Red	1 spool
◄	Kreinik #16 Braid	008C	Light Green	1 spool
●	Madeira Glamour	2458	Dark Green	1 spool
▽	Kreinik #16 Braid	052HL	Dark Brown	1 spool
▬	Kreinik #16 Braid	202HL	Gold	1 spool

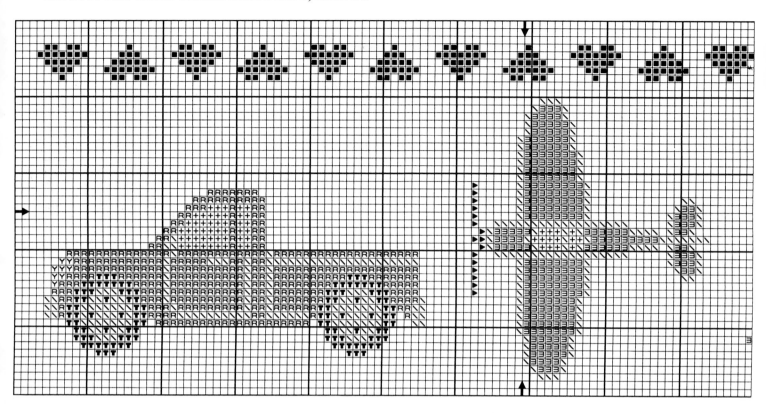

COLOR KEY

Symbol	Fiber Name	Number	Color	Amount
+	DMC Cotton Floss	Blanc	White	1 skein
∃	DMC Cotton Floss	798	French Blue	1 skein
R	DMC Cotton Floss	349	Red	1 skein
T	Kreinik 1/16 ribbon	005	Black	1 spool
■	Madeira Glamour	2415	Dark Red	1 spool
\	Anchor Marlitt	845	Grey	1 skein
▶	Kreinik 1/16 ribbon	225C	Dark Grey	1 spool
Y	Anchor Marlitt	821	Yellow	1 skein

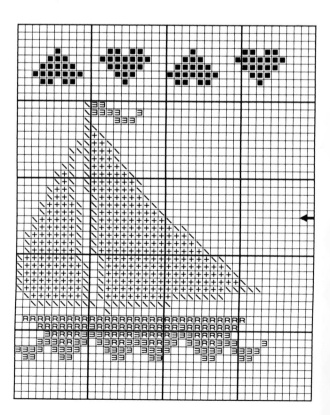

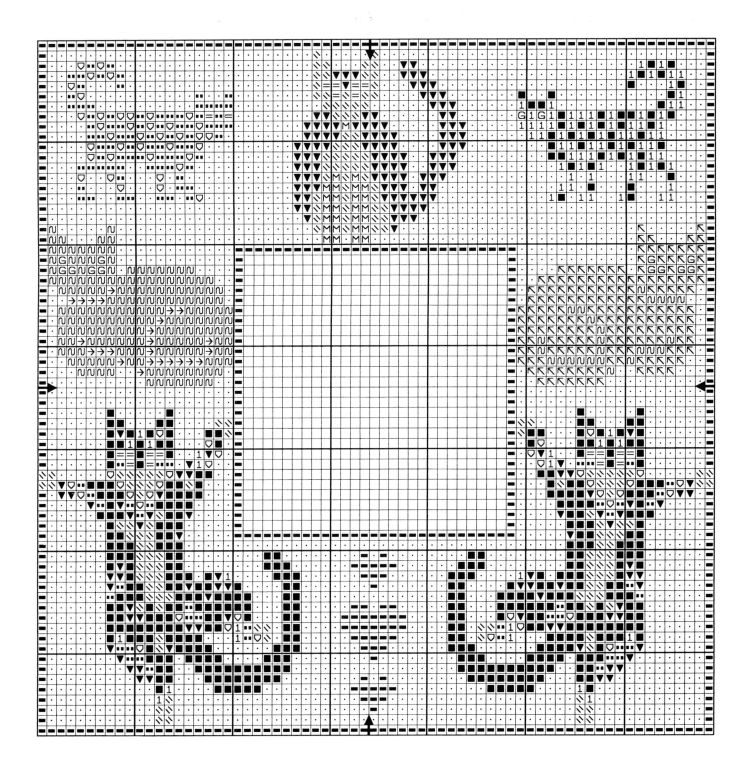

COLOR KEY

Symbol	Fiber Name	Number	Color	Amount
■	Anchor #3 Perle	236	Dark Grey	1 skein
1	Anchor #3 Perle	393	Dark Buff	1 skein
◣	Anchor #3 Perle	926	White	1 skein
▬	Madeira Glamour	2415	Dark Red	1 spool
=	Kreinik #16 Braid	008C	Green	1 spool
·	Paternayan Persian	220	Black	40 yds. (36 m)
M	Anchor #3 Perle	388	Light Buff	1 skein
◤	Anchor #3 Perle	235	Light Grey	1 skein
→	Anchor #3 Perle	920	Light Slate	1 skein
∏	Anchor #3 Perle	922	Dark Slate	1 skein
▽	Anchor #3 Perle	366	Light Apricot	1 skein
∙∙	Anchor #3 Perle	369	Medium Apricot	1 skein
▼	Anchor #3 Perle	936	Dark Apricot	1 skein
G	Kreinik #16 Braid	202HL	Gold	1 spool

Enlarge pattern 150%

Index of Projects and Expressions